THE FRUIT OF THE SPIRIT

Maturing Into the Likeness of Christ

By

Doretha McBride

The Fruit of the Spirit

Maturing into the Likeness of Christ

Copyright © 2022 by Doretha McBride

All Rights Reserved.

Edited, formatted, and published by

Destiny House Publishing, LLC.

P.O. Box 19774

Detroit, MI 48219

inquiry@destinyhousepublishing.com

www.destinyhousepublishing.com

404.993.0830

Cover by Kingdom Graphic Designs

This work may not be used in any form, or reproduced by any means, in whole or in part, without written permission from the publisher or author. Unless otherwise stated, all scripture is from the Amplified Bible (AMP). Printed in the United States

ISBN: 978-1-936867-82-0

Table of Contents

Introduction v

Chapter 1- Love: The First Fruit 1

Chapter 2- Joy: That Delightful Fruit 19

Chapter 3- Peace: The Sabbath Fruit 30

Chapter 4- Longsuffering: The Merciful Fruit 42

Chapter 5- Gentleness: The Sweet Fruit 54

Chapter 6- Goodness: The Ethical Fruit 65

Chapter 7- Faith: The Fruit of Agreement 75

Chapter 8- Faith Walkers 88

Chapter 9- Meekness: The Fruit of Humility 108

Chapter 10- Temperance: The Fruit of Insurance 119

Chapter 11- OK! What's Next? 132

About the Author 138

INTRODUCTION

Matthew 7:16-20 (NASB) ¹⁶ You will know them by their fruits. Grapes are not gathered from thorn bushes, nor figs from thistles, are they? ¹⁷ So every good tree bears good fruit, but the bad tree bears bad fruit. ¹⁸ A good tree cannot bear bad fruit, nor can a bad tree bear good fruit. ¹⁹ Every tree that does not bear good fruit is cut down and thrown into the fire. ²⁰ So then, you will know them by their fruits.

Too many of us stand in the shadows, peeping around the curtains, watching as God demonstrates larger-than-life events and even small miracles occur of which we desire to be a part. God is dynamic, always moving and doing things, showing Himself strong and capable of doing great things. These things function to let us see into His character and to increase our faith and trust in Him. We begin to wonder why we are not a part of these events and why we choose to stay in the shadows. And we know we should be, and actually want to be, active in His plan for our lives.

But something hinders our progress, so we hide from His light on the sidelines. What is this *thing*, or these *things*, which get in our way? They are the lies that we have believed about ourselves, and even about God. Satan, the enemy of our souls, is extremely good at planting the same types of seeds that he planted in Eve in the Garden of Eden. He indicated to Eve that God did not want His best for her, so He was withholding it from her. He tells us that we don't have what it takes to come into God's marvelous light. And we won't have to face that rejection that has become so familiar in our lives if we stay safely behind the curtain. Of course, if we don't do it, someone else will so "Why should I get involved?" He tells us that this is true humility. These lies cause us to shake behind the curtain in fear and shame, while we long to be noticed. And then there are those of us who want to operate in the gifts but have not prepared the foundation necessary to be effective. We have not done the work to be in a position to bear fruit.

Let me talk about this curtain that we believe protects us. It is a place where we can stay under the radar, and no one can challenge us to do the very things we desire to do for the Lord. It is meant to prevent exposure to the sins that so easily besets us. It deceives us into believing that we can hide behind it. It's the place that keeps us safe from the assignment of purpose for which God predestined us. After all, it's scary dealing with the prospect of living fearlessly like Jesus lived. Living in that place makes us prime targets for ridicule and persecution. Okay, I'll give you that part. Walking with Jesus and doing the work that He has called us to can be a bit scary. But behind that curtain is a place of darkness. It's meant to keep us from the light of the Lord. Jesus left Holy Spirit with us, so we are *never alone*. And to be perfectly honest, walking with Him is the safest place that we

Introduction

could find ourselves. And we really do want to shine for the One whose glorious light shone for us.

Stepping into the light with Jesus is worth the risk of any perceived short-term discomfort in this life. Many things we think will be painful will actually become the things that draw us nearer to Him. There is nothing more satisfying than walking in the light of the Lord and shining brightly for His glory! So, answer each one His calls without hesitation!

Apostle John tells us just why this is important.

John 15:16-17 *[16] Ye have not chosen me, but I have chosen you, and ordained you, that ye should go and bring forth fruit, and that your fruit should remain: that whatsoever ye shall ask of the Father in my name, he may give it you. [17] These things I command you, that ye love one another.*

Apostle Paul taught about the fruit of the Spirit vs the fruit of the flesh because there were issues in Galatia - much false teaching in the new churches - and confusion was beginning to set in. Jewish leaders wanted the Galatians to live by the law rather than by grace, by tradition rather than by faith in Christ and the work he did on the cross. So, Paul had to address the behaviors he was seeing that resulted from the legalism being taught.

Galatians 5:16-21 *[16] This I say then, Walk in the Spirit, and ye shall not fulfil the lust of the flesh. [17] For the flesh lusteth against the Spirit,* *and the Spirit against the flesh: and these are contrary the one to the other: so that ye cannot do the things that ye would. ¹⁸ But if ye be led of the Spirit, ye are not under the law. ¹⁹ Now the works of the flesh are manifest, which are these; Adultery, fornication, uncleanness, lasciviousness, ²⁰ Idolatry, witchcraft, hatred, variance, emulations, wrath, strife, seditions, heresies, ²¹ Envyings, murders, drunkenness, revellings, and such like: of the which I tell you before, as I have also told you in time past, that they which do such things shall not inherit the kingdom of God.*

The flesh is our old human nature that we inherited with the curse of sin received in the Garden of Eden. It was passed down through generations to our parents, entwined with self-centeredness and habitual sin. We must <u>crucify the flesh</u> and stay connected to the true vine in order to walk in the fruit of the Spirit! And we certainly do not want God to cut us off because we refuse to resist that flesh nature.

John 15:1-7 *¹ "I am the true Vine, and My Father is the vinedresser. ² Every branch in Me that does not bear fruit, He takes away; and every branch that continues to bear fruit, He [repeatedly] prunes, so that it will bear more fruit [even richer and finer fruit]. ³ You are already clean because of the word which I have given you [the teachings which I have discussed with you]. ⁴ Remain in Me, and I in you. Just as the branch cannot bear fruit of itself but must remain in the vine, so neither can you unless you remain in Me. ⁵ I am the vine, you are the branches; the one who remains in Me, and I in him bears*

Introduction

much fruit, for apart from Me you can do nothing. ⁶ If anyone does not remain in Me, he is thrown away like a branch and dries up; and they gather them and throw them into the fire, and they are burned. ⁷ If you remain in Me, and My words remain in you, ask whatever you wish, and it will be done for you.

Paul admonishes us to live things with the help of Holy Spirit, to live by the fruit of the Spirit instead of that of the flesh.

Galatians 5:22-25 *²² But the fruit of the Spirit is love, joy, peace, longsuffering, gentleness, goodness, faith, ²³ Meekness, temperance: against such there is no law. ²⁴ And they that are Christ's have crucified the flesh with the affections and lusts. ²⁵ If we live in the Spirit, let us also walk in the Spirit.*

Notice, there are almost twice as many works of the flesh than works of the Spirit! So, we must work twice as hard to practice the fruit of the Spirit than we do to demonstrate the works of the flesh.

In this book, I want to address the call to *mature into Christlikeness* by bearing spiritual fruit. I'll be presenting a myriad of scriptures, all from the Amplified version of the Bible, unless otherwise noted. But it is my goal to teach on the fruit of the Spirit so that we can live life by the Spirit. Without the fruit of the Spirit, our gifts will not be effective. These are the principles whereby we should be living if we want to be used by God! Here, I will try to offer a few guidelines. And as you meditate on the journaling at the end of each chapter, let Holy

Spirit shine His light and speak to your hearts, prune every broken place, and prepare you to produce more fruit than you could have ever imagined.

I promise this…it's not too late! Peace and Blessings!

Introduction

CHAPTER ONE
LOVE: THE FIRST FRUIT

Love is mentioned approximately 541 times in the Bible. I call love the first fruit because I believe it is the *best gift* that we can give to God. Just as we give our first fruit offerings, love is exactly that, an offering to God. Love is genuine, unselfish concern for another. This can be a mate, a friend, or a family member. It is a loyalty beyond that which we have toward those we do not know, yet it should also be extended to them. It is representative of the Love that God has for us and how we should feel toward Him. God loves us and we were created to reciprocate that love to Him and others. We show that we love Him by obeying Him and showing His love to others.

Matthew 22:36-40 [36] *"Teacher, which is the greatest commandment in the Law?"* [37] *And Jesus replied to him, "'YOU SHALL LOVE THE LORD YOUR GOD WITH ALL YOUR HEART, AND WITH ALL YOUR SOUL, AND WITH ALL YOUR MIND.'* [38] *This is the first and greatest commandment.* [39] *The second is like it, 'YOU SHALL LOVE YOUR NEIGHBOR AS YOURSELF [that is, unselfishly seek the best or higher good for others].'* [40] *The whole Law and the [writings of the] Prophets depend on these two commandments."*

Everything prophesied to us in the Word depends on us loving God with all our hearts, souls, and minds, while also loving others as we do ourselves. Mark 12:30, Luke 10:27 adds ... *'with all your strength.'* Holy Spirit downloads love into us but we must have hearts open to His impartation.

Romans 5:5 *Such hope [in God's promises] never disappoints us, because God's love has been abundantly poured out within our hearts through the Holy Spirit who was given to us.*

This is the greatest test we will have as Christians because love is critically interrelated with having enough faith to obey God. A faith that does not manifest itself in obedience and love toward God and man is dead and worthless. Obedience is proof that we love God.

1 John 5:3-4 *³This is love for God: to obey his commands. And his commands are not burdensome, ⁴for everyone born of God overcomes the world.*

James 2:26 *For just as the [human] body without the spirit is dead, so faith without works [of obedience] is also dead.*

Galatians 5:6 *For [if we are] in Christ Jesus neither circumcision nor uncircumcision means anything, but only faith activated and expressed and working through love.*

2 John:6 *And this is love: that we walk in obedience to his commands. As you have heard from the beginning, his command is that you walk in love. But this love is incompatible with love of the world.*

Father expects us to first love Him. Without our love for Him, we cannot love ourselves enough to truly love others. But how can I love God the way He desires? We must allow Holy Spirit to circumcise your hearts and shed His love abroad in it. This is not a circumcision of the hands, but one of the Spirit.

Romans *2:28-29* *²⁸ For he is not a [real] Jew who is only one outwardly, nor is [true] circumcision something external and physical. ²⁹ But he is a Jew who is one inwardly; and [true] circumcision is circumcision of the heart, by the Spirit, not by [the fulfillment of] the letter [of the Law]. His praise is not from men, but from God.*

We can only love and worship one God, otherwise we are operating in duplicity. The fact of the matter is that we are only created to commit to one love.

Matthew 6:24 *"No one can serve two masters; for either he will hate the one and love the other, or he will be devoted to the one and despise the other. You cannot serve God and mammon [money, possessions, fame, status, or whatever is valued more than the Lord].*

So actually, we are either worshipping God or Satan. Father God has much more to say about worshipping other gods (see Deuteronomy).

We are also to love others as we love ourselves. Christians are always saying how we want to be free, meaning we don't want to be bound and limited by ourselves or anyone else! But God's freedom refers to having no limitations in our ability to be devoted to Him. It's never about independence from God, but obedience to Him. It's the ability to make right decisions for the right reasons. Notice, it is the *ability* to make right decisions in demonstrating His love. Paul says we are to use this freedom to serve one another throu love.

Galatians 5:13-14 [13] *For, brethren, ye have been called unto liberty; only use not liberty for an occasion to the flesh, but by love serve one another.* [14] *For all the law is fulfilled in one word, even in this; Thou shalt love thy neighbor as thyself.*

Now I think this would be making a right decision, don't you? But do you love yourself? Love is defined as affectionate concern for the well-being of others. This means you! You must be concerned for your own well-being before you can be concerned for another.

I'm not talking about self-centeredness here. I'm talking about true God-centeredness meaning all you want for yourself is what God wants for you...*meaning you will go against yourself to please God*...meaning you take care of yourself spiritually, physically, mentally, emotionally, and financially according to His will.

Spiritual care means that you study the Word, live a saved lifestyle as revealed by the Word, attend corporate services ready to participate and with the expectation of building your knowledge and faith, be passionate about producing fruit for God, trust that God is working things out in your life and be patient enough to wait on him to fix it, and come to know that God will not, actually ***cannot***, fail you!

Physical care means that you eat right, exercise, go to the doctor when needed, and see to it that you look good as a representative of God! This includes being dressed appropriately as not to distract from the light of the Lord.

Mental and emotional care involves renewing your mind daily with God's Word, meditating on that Word, confessing the Word over yourself, and thinking good thoughts.

Philippians 4:8 *Finally, believers, whatever is true, whatever is honorable and worthy of respect, whatever is right and confirmed by God's word, whatever is pure and wholesome, whatever is lovely and brings peace, whatever is admirable and of good repute; if there is any excellence, if there is anything worthy of praise, think continually on these things [center your mind on them, and implant them in your heart].*

We must also have someone in your life with whom you can be accountable, completely honest to share your overwhelming thoughts.

James 5:16 *Therefore, confess your sins to one another [your false steps, your offenses], and pray for one another, that you may be healed and restored. The heartfelt and persistent prayer of a righteous man (believer) can accomplish much [when put into action and made effective by God—it is dynamic and can have tremendous power].*

Take off the masks!! Be humble enough to share with someone and give it all to Jesus for He cares for you.

1 Peter 5:6-7 *⁶ Therefore humble yourselves under the mighty hand of God [set aside self-righteous pride], so that He may exalt you [to a place of honor in His service] at the appropriate time, ⁷ casting all your cares [all your anxieties, all your worries, and all your concerns, once and for all] on Him, for He cares about you [with deepest affection, and watches over you very carefully].*

Finally, financial care means that you pay your tithes, give your offerings, sow into the lives of others, pay your bills and taxes, and do not create new debt! Love yourself enough to do this so you can show love by giving to others! The loving care for the wellbeing of others is serious to God.

When we think of charity, we think of some generous actions or donations to aid and assist the poor, ill, helpless, elderly, unnoticed, and others.

Matthew 25:34-40 *³⁴ "Then the King will say to those on His right, 'Come, you blessed of My Father [you favored of God, appointed to eternal salvation], inherit the kingdom prepared for you from the foundation of the world. ³⁵ For I was hungry, and you gave Me something to eat; I was thirsty, and you gave Me something to drink; I was a stranger, and you invited Me in; ³⁶ I was naked, and you clothed Me; I was sick, and you visited Me [with help and ministering care]; I was in prison, and you came to Me [ignoring personal danger].' ³⁷ Then the righteous will answer Him, 'Lord, when did we see You hungry, and feed You, or thirsty, and give You something to drink? ³⁸ And when did we see You as a stranger, and invite You in, or* *naked, and clothe You?* *³⁹ And when did we see You sick, or in prison, and come to You?' ⁴⁰ The King will answer and say to them, 'I assure you and most solemnly say to you, to the extent that you did it for one of these brothers of Mine, even the least of them, you did it for Me.'*

But there's more! Paul tells us what we look like when we don't show love to others. As I said before, this brotherly love is so serious to God, He had Paul write an entire chapter, 1 Corinthians 13, to clarify what real love for others looks like. But in the first three verses, he wrote about what it does *not* look like.

1 Corinthians 13:1-3 *¹ If I speak with the tongues of men and of angels, but have not love [for others growing out of God's love for me], then I have become only a noisy gong or a clanging cymbal [just an annoying distraction]. ² And if I have the gift of prophecy [and speak a new message from God to the people], and understand all mysteries, and [possess] all knowledge; and if I have all [sufficient] faith so that I can remove mountains, but do not have love [reaching out to others], I am nothing. ³ If I give all my possessions to feed the poor, and if I surrender my body to be burned, but do not have love, it does me no good at all.*

He is not just talking about taking care of the poor, the sick, the orphans, the widows, or those imprisoned in body or mind. He is speaking of the attitude with which we do it. And if it's not an attitude of love, it's just like making a loud noise…and effectively ineffective!!

I can prophesy until I'm blue in the face, have great revelation, and have more faith than anyone you have ever seen, but I'm nobody, worthless to God, without love!!! I can be the greatest giver, giving more than anyone I know, but there will be no reward, no increase, without love!!!!! So, what is love for real? Paul tells us in verses 4 through 8.

⁴ Love endures with patience and serenity, love is kind and thoughtful, and is not jealous or envious; love does not brag and is not proud or arrogant.

Love can be *patient and serene*! It can wait for a change to come. It endures delay, hardship, annoyance, pain, provocation, and persecution with strength, consistency, and serenity (calmness), and without complaint, anger, or frustration. We must be patient with God, ourselves, and others! We will always show impatience with others when we are impatient with ourselves! Say, "Lord, help us all!"

And love is kind and thoughtful. It is good in temperament, considerate, helpful, and gracious, meaning it's full of the manifestation of favor, compassion, or forgiveness. It **quickly** lets go of offense!!

Love is not jealous or envious. So, it does not feel discontent or covetous when witnessing or hearing of another person's anointing, gifts, advantages, successes, or possessions. There's no competition in love!! Wow! What a concept for some!

We should only want the gift God has for us. We've all been assigned at least one. And remember, they all originate from God so if you don't have it, maybe it's not your gift or you are not ready for it. Whatever the case, seek God. But no competitive coveting.

Proverbs 14:30 *A calm **and** peaceful **and** tranquil heart is life **and** health to the body, but passion **and** envy are like rottenness to the bones.*

Love does not brag. It does not speak with exaggeration or excessive pride, especially about oneself. That thing you think is superior to others is usually something that's just *in your own mind, anyway* and no one notices it, but you. God promised, if we humble ourselves, he will exalt us in due season. It is a selfish and prideful thing to boast!

Love is not proud or arrogant. It is not shared in a way that exhibits an inordinate or high opinion of your own self-perceived importance. God hates pride!!!

[5] It is not rude; it is not self-seeking; it is not provoked [nor overly sensitive and easily angered]; it does not take into account a wrong endured.

Love is not rude, discourteous, or impolite. It is not harsh or insensitive, just because we are in a bad mood. It is needful to be on alert for those 'bad moments, or days'. It doesn't ignore people or pretend they are non-existent through exclusion. It will even be kind to rude people who have a bad attitude.

LOVE is not self-seeking. It is not selfish or self-centered because it is always thinking of others. It is not manipulative, deceitful, or sneaky for personal gain! Love doesn't need instant gratification because it wants what is best, not what is easiest!

LOVE is not easily provoked, overly sensitive, or easily angered, offended, irritated. These reactions cause stress which can lead to a multitude of illnesses, such as hypertension, depression, and even cancer! In contrast, real love obeys God as he commands in Psalm 34:14…Turn away from evil and do good; seek peace and pursue it. In order to do this, we must forgive quickly!

Love does not take into account a wrong endured. It does not keep a record of perceived wrongs done by others and it does not hold resentments. Leviticus 19:18 *Do not seek revenge or bear a grudge against one of your people, but love your neighbor as yourself.* This is almost impossible in this selfish age. It's even difficult for the believer. But the love of God will forgive quickly because we all need forgiveness. And we receive forgiveness in the same way that we forgive others (Matthew 6:12).

[6] *It does not rejoice at injustice, but rejoices with the truth [when right and truth prevail].*

Love does not find pleasure in evil behavior or the punishment of others. Love is not happy to hear bad news about someone just because we don't like them. That's just demonic! You may ask, "What about those who have constantly hurt us?" I believe that we must put our flesh under subjection and just do it as an act of our will until our feelings catch up with our desire to please God. But know those who labor among you!

Love: The First Fruit

⁷ Love bears all things [regardless of what comes], believes all things [looking for the best in each one], hopes all things [remaining steadfast during difficult times], endures all things [without weakening].

Love bears all things regardless of what happens. It always supports and protects others. It never exposes them, but it covers a multitude of sins and keeps the confidence of others. Can you keep a confidence – a secret that is confided trustfully to you - or do you just have to tell your mate, friend, or somebody? Just asking (smile)?

But love will hold up under pressure, even when you feel betrayed, disrespected, or ignored. It bears up under all of the things that love is not!! It hangs in there!

Love believes all things looking for the best in everyone. See, real love first seeks good of and in everyone. It has a confident expectation of other's good motives. It always expects others to exhibit good character and to get better. So, there is no need to gossip or spread rumors, especially about their personal or private issues, or about how bad *you* think they are! But is it gossip to speak to God or your pastor about a person's business when it directly affects you? Absolutely not! But watch your motives!

Ask yourself, what can I admire about this person? Is there anything that is praiseworthy about them? Then tell yourself," That's what I will choose to think about!"

Love hopes all things, remaining steadfast during difficult times. It always anticipates the best with confidence that God will bring good to pass in their lives. Love never doubts, loses faith, or shuts down. Love is hopeful expectation of God's will in, for, and through yourself and others!!!!!

Love endures all things without weakening. It always perseveres and continues steadfastly. It sustains and holds up to resistance patiently, without yielding. It presses through hard times; it "takes a licking and keeps on ticking" (Timex). It tolerates inconveniences. It maintains its purpose in spite of discouragement, difficulties, or obstacles. It remains in the relationship as long as there is no abuse. Let me make this perfectly clear! It is not the will of God that we be abused in any manner.

Otherwise, fight hard for your God-given relationships. Hear me clearly. There may be some relationships that you do not believe are worth fighting for. But all God-given relationships are worth the fight. Again, you may ask, "How can I endure the pain of what they did?" Well, first be sure that you have forgiven them. And then realize that God will be on the side of the righteous, and with that, you can handle whatever you face!

[8] *Love never fails [it never fades nor ends]. But as for prophecies, they will pass away; as for tongues, they will cease; as for the gift of special knowledge, it will pass away.*

Love never fails, fades, or ends. Even when we must remove people from our lives, we can still love them. Real love never always wins, even when it appears to fail. It never decreases or disappears. It endures until the end!!!!!

1 John 4:18 *There is no fear in love [dread does not exist]. But perfect (complete, full-grown) love drives out fear, because fear involves [the expectation of divine] punishment, so the one who is afraid [of God's judgment] is not perfected in love [has not grown into a sufficient understanding of God's love].*

This means fear of needs not being met, rejection, abandonment, or embarrassment will prevent this kind of love. It's a perfect, mature love that casts out all fear of being hurt, allowing you to take down your walls.

Again, we are not expected to put ourselves in harm's way or in danger to really love someone. But according to Romans 13:8, we owe no man anything, but to love one another: for he that loveth another hath fulfilled the law. So, loving others is a nonnegotiable command. It matters not if they are Saints or sinners, we must love!

That's why 1 Corinthians 13:8 ends telling us tongues will cease and gifts of special knowledge will pass away but love lasts forever. So, we must mature into the perfect love of 1 John 4:18 that casts out all fear of hurt and torment because our trust and confidence is in the Lord who cannot fail us or leave us ashamed.

I believe that love is the first fruit written about because, in my humble opinion, I believe the definition, as described in 1 Corinthians 13:4-8, of love includes all of the other fruit as follows:

- JOY (vs 6,7): when we love, we rejoice in all things and believe for the best in others.

- PEACE (vs 7): when we love, we have hope which brings peace,

- LONGSUFFERING (vs 4,7): when we love, we are more patient.

- GENTLENESS (vs 4): when we love, we are kind to others.

- GOODNESS (vs 4,7): when we love, we bear other's burdens without exposing or judging,

- FAITH (vs 7): when we love, we believe for and seek the best in others, trusting God so we can be faithful.

- MEEKNESS (vs 5): when we love, we are not easily provoked.

- TEMPERANCE (vs 6): when we love, we can endure patiently.

Psalm 133:1-3 [1] *How good and pleasant it is when brothers live together in unity!* [2] *It is like precious oil poured on the head, running down on the beard, running down on Aaron's beard, down upon the collar of his robes.* [3] *It is as if the dew of Hermon were falling on Mount Zion. For there the LORD bestows his blessing, even life forevermore.*

Love: The First Fruit

Now if the Aaron was refreshed by unity, then everyone should be blessed by it. And you can imagine how God feels about it! It is because love is the most excellent way! There is no "I", only "we", in the love of Jesus. When there is an "I" mentality, there is separation from the body of Christ and there is disconnection from the True Vine.

Of course, we know, we can't do any of this unless we first love God. So, let's submit to Holy Spirit so that He can shed God's love in our hearts and we can exhibit the fruit of love! Hard? Maybe! But we still are commanded to love so how about we just do it!!!!!

My prayers are with each reader as I write this!

TIME TO MEDITATE ON IT

Romans 13:9 *The commandments, "You shall not commit adultery, you shall not murder, you shall not steal, you shall not covet," and any other commandment are summed up in this statement: "You shall love your neighbor as yourself."*

How is your love walk? When studying 1 Corinthians 13, in which areas can you improve? What steps can you take, starting today?

_____

_____

_____

_____

_____

_____

_____

_____

_____

_____

_____

_____

_____

_____

Love: The First Fruit

1 Corinthians 8:2-3 *²The man who thinks he knows something does not yet know as he ought to know. ³But the man who loves God is known by God.*

CHAPTER TWO
JOY: THAT DELIGHTFUL FRUIT

Psalm 13:5-6 *5 But I have trusted and relied on and been confident in Your lovingkindness and faithfulness; My heart shall rejoice and delight in Your salvation. 6 I will sing to the Lord, Because He has dealt bountifully with me.*

Joy is the expression of contentment or manifestation of intense, ecstatic, triumphant pleasure. This is why I call it 'that delightful fruit.' It occurs when we take delight in someone and we are genuinely grateful for having been in their presence. But it's more than a feeling. It's a state of mind and a way of being, regardless of circumstances. But this can't be done unless we walk in the love of God mentioned in I Corinthians 13 because… "Stuff happens!" God warns us to prepare our hearts for this 'stuff' by knowing Who He is in our lives.

Habakkuk 3:17-19 [17] *Though the fig tree does not blossom And there is no fruit on the vines, Though the yield of the olive fails And the fields produce no food, Though the flock is cut off from the fold and there* *are no cattle in the stalls, ¹⁸ Yet I will [choose to] rejoice in the Lord; I will [choose to] shout in exultation in the [victorious] God of my salvation! ¹⁹ The Lord God is my strength [my source of courage, my invincible army]; He has made my feet [steady and sure] like hinds' feet And makes me walk [forward with spiritual confidence] on my high places [of challenge and responsibility].*

We must know without a doubt that Our Savior and Lord will strengthen us and enable us to walk in enduring love, in *all* situations.

Psalm 19:8 *The precepts of the Lord are right, bringing joy to the heart; The commandment of the Lord is pure, enlightening the eyes.*

God's ways give light to our eyes. So, if we surrender and do life His way, He is in it, and we will have the power to stand! When we have this mindset, our joy will be sustained and remain!

Philippians 4:4 *Rejoice in the Lord always [delight, take pleasure in Him]; again I will say, rejoice!*

Who are we rejoicing in? **THE LORD**! And how often should we rejoice? **Always**!

Rejoice means to feel joyful, be delighted, or to hold dear.

In what do you find yourself rejoicing, taking delight in, or holding dear? A raise? Your children's good grades? A new car or nice gift? Money? Your talents? Your reputation? Your accomplishments? How about we focus on rejoicing in the Lord, first and foremost? Why? There are many reasons; but here are some good ones!

Matthew 6:33 *But first and most importantly seek (aim at, strive after) His kingdom and His righteousness [His way of doing and being right—the attitude and character of God], and all these things will be given to you also.*

Psalm 16:11 *You have made known to me the path of life; you will fill me with joy in your presence, with eternal pleasures at your right hand. There IS JOY in the presence of the Lord! And Nehemiah 8:10b ... the joy of the LORD is your strength."*

Psalm 94:19 *When my anxious thoughts multiply within me, Your comforts delight me.*

God's promises never fail. One promise is that if we seek His kingdom and His righteous way of doing things first, He will provide all these things…and more. If we seek Him, we will find Him. And when we find Him, in His presence we will also find fullness of joy. Even when we are full of anxiety, He will not only console us, but He will bring to us delightful joy. So, we can have joy in doing the will of God, even when "Stuff happens!"

We should also find joy in our ability to give because, if we can give, God must be blessing us. He loves a cheerful giver, and He gives seed to the sower, right? (2 Corinthians 9:6-15). So, we should be happy to sow! And not only will we find joy in giving, but others will be filled with joy by our generosity and bless God the Father.

Deuteronomy 12:6-7 *⁶there bring your burnt offerings and sacrifices, your tithes and special gifts, what you have vowed to give and your* *freewill offerings, and the firstborn of your herds and flocks.* [7] *There, in the presence of the LORD your God, you and your families shall eat and shall rejoice in everything you have put your hand to, because the LORD your God has blessed you.*

I am sure that you can identify times in your life that you felt joy because you chose to do the right thing. We should always find joy when we, as God's people, do the righteous thing because 1 Chronicles 29:17 tells us that He tests our hearts and is pleased when we walk in integrity. I'll talk more about that in Chapter 6. And Romans 16:19 tells us that the word is spread when we walk in obedience. This brings God joy so it should bring us joy as well!

We should find joy when God's kingdom work is being done.

Ezra 3:11 *They sang [responsively], praising and giving thanks to the Lord, saying, "For He is good, for His lovingkindness (mercy) toward Israel endures forever." And all the people shouted with a great shout when they praised the Lord because the foundation of the house of the Lord was laid.*

Seeing the kingdom of God built, by His blueprint, should produce a praise and thankfulness that is an expression of our joy! We should be ecstatically joyful whenever kingdom work is being accomplished, whether it is our ministry or another ministry! Our ministry was extremely excited when we walked into The Life Center of New Destiny Ministries in Merrillville, Indiana. Although this apostolic center, overseen by Larry and Torrona Tillman, was not something that we ourselves had done, it was something that God had done for their ministry! This is the mindset that we must have in God's kingdom. It doesn't matter who is doing it. Again, there should be no competition or coveting in the kingdom. It only matters that it gets done for the glory of Jesus.

Our ministry is an outreach ministry. We love coming alongside other ministries with similar visions to build the house of the Lord, His Church, His Bride. We also come alongside ministries who provide other types of services for the work of kingdom building. I believe, this is the will of God concerning us.

We must have joy even in the hard times. Here's how God sees it.

1 Peter 4:12-14 *12 Beloved do not be surprised at the fiery ordeal which is taking place to test you [that is, to test the quality of your faith], as though something strange or unusual were happening to you. 13 But insofar as you are sharing Christ's sufferings, keep on rejoicing, so that when His glory [filled with His radiance and splendor] is revealed, you may rejoice with great joy. 14 If you are insulted and reviled for [bearing] the name of Christ, you are blessed [happy, with life-joy and comfort in God's salvation regardless of your circumstances], because the Spirit of glory and of God is resting on you [and indwelling you—He whom they curse, you glorify].*

Matthew 5:11-12 *11 "Blessed [morally courageous and spiritually alive with life-joy in God's goodness] are you when people insult you and persecute you, and falsely say all kinds of evil things against you because of [your association with] Me. 12 Be glad and exceedingly joyful, for your reward in heaven is great [absolutely* *inexhaustible]; for in this same way they persecuted the prophets who were before you.*

When we live for the Lord and expect to produce fruit, we should expect to suffer and to be talked about, insulted, or tempted to 'snap'. We're right there on the edge of the cliff even though we know the Word! But we also know that we will be blessed if we suffer well. Yep, we are told to be joyful in its midst because our reward is certain. These are times when we *must* repeat scriptures like Psalm 51:12 *Restore to me the joy of Your salvation And sustain me with a willing spirit.* And confess Psalm 13:5-6 *⁵ But I have trusted and relied on and been confident in Your lovingkindness and faithfulness; My heart shall rejoice and delight in Your salvation. ⁶ I will sing to the Lord, Because He has dealt bountifully with me.* Soon you'll actually be singing, Psalm 30:11 *You have turned my mourning into dancing for me; You have taken off my sackcloth and clothed me with joy.*

Prophesy over yourself:

Isaiah 61:10 *I will rejoice greatly in the Lord, My soul will exult in my God; For He has clothed me with garments of salvation, He has covered me with a robe of righteousness, As a bridegroom puts on a turban, And as a bride adorns herself with her jewels.*

Psalm 118:24 *This is the day the LORD has made; let us rejoice and be glad in it.*

But the best reason to rejoice and remain full of joy is that we know that one day, we will be married to the Lamb of God!

Revelation 19:6-7 *⁶ Then I heard something like the shout of a vast multitude, and like the boom of many pounding waves, and like the roar of mighty peals of thunder, saying, "Hallelujah! For the Lord our God, the Almighty, [the Omnipotent, the Ruler of all] reigns. ⁷ Let us rejoice and shout for joy! Let us give Him glory and honor, for the marriage of the Lamb has come [at last] and His bride (the redeemed) has prepared herself."*

So, rejoice in the Lord always. I will say it again: Rejoice!

Finally, let's talk about the joy of a grateful heart. Again, joy is the expression of contentment or manifestation of intense, ecstatic, triumphant pleasure. And we know it's more than a feeling.... it's a state of mind.... a way of being, regardless of circumstances.

Psalm 138 *¹I will praise thee with my whole heart: before the gods will I sing praise unto thee. ² I will worship toward thy holy temple, and praise thy name for thy lovingkindness and for thy truth: for thou hast magnified thy word above all thy name.*

Psalm 30:1, 4-7, 11-12 *¹I will extol thee, O LORD; for thou hast lifted me up, and hast not made my foes to rejoice over me. ⁴Sing unto the LORD, O ye saints of his, and give thanks at the remembrance of his holiness. ⁵For his anger endureth but a moment; in his favor is life: weeping may endure for a night, but joy cometh in the morning. ⁶And in my prosperity I said, I shall never be moved. ⁷LORD, by thy favor* *thou hast made my mountain to stand strong: thou didst hide thy face, and I was troubled. ¹¹Thou hast turned for me my mourning into dancing: thou hast put off my sackcloth, and girded me with gladness; ¹²To the end that my glory may sing praise to thee, and not be silent. O LORD my God, I will give thanks unto thee forever. The Message Bible ¹ I give you all the credit, GOD— you got me out of that mess, you didn't let my foes gloat. ⁴⁻⁵ All you saints! Sing your hearts out to GOD! Thank him to his face! He gets angry once in a while, but across a lifetime there is only love. The nights of crying your eyes out give way to days of laughter. ⁶⁻⁷ When things were going great I crowed, "I've got it made. I'm GOD's favorite. He made me king of the mountain." Then you looked the other way and I fell to pieces. ¹¹⁻¹² You did it: you changed wild lament into whirling dance; You ripped off my black mourning band and decked me with wildflowers. I'm about to burst with song; I can't keep quiet about you. God, my God, I can't thank you enough.*

So, let's remember, God can turn your weeping into dancing; weeping may endure for a night, but joy cometh in the morning. As you praise Him today, exhibit your fruit and give Him a sacrificial shout of *joy!*

TIME TO MEDITATE ON IT

Isaiah 61:3 *Our Lord has given us beauty for ashes, the oil of joy for mourning, the garment of praise for the Spirit of heaviness; that we might be called trees of righteousness, the planting of the LORD, that God might be glorified.*

How much joy do you have in your daily life? For what can you say that you're grateful? Start making a gratitude list to find joy in your day!

_____

_____

_____

_____

_____

_____

_____

_____

_____

_____

_____

_____

_____

_____

Psalm 47:1 *O clap your hands, all ye people; shout unto God with the voice of triumph.*

Joy: That Delightful Fruit

CHAPTER THREE
PEACE: THE SABBATH FRUIT

It is important to understand the correlation between rest and our level of peace. When I am overly tired, I tend to overthink and get irritable very quickly for no good reason. It can even lead to depressive episodes. When dealing with others, those behaviors are intolerable. Lack of rest or peace can destroy relationships.

Peace is a state of mutual harmony. It is a state of tranquility, serenity, and contentment. In the Old Testament, it indicated freedom from disturbance, whether outwardly from enemies or from within. The Hebrew word is 'shalom' and it basically means prosperity, security from enemies, and general wellbeing or good standing with man and God. When you were greeted with 'shalom,' you were being given their primary form of blessing. In the New Testament, it is primarily indicative of a spiritual condition of contentment from and with God. It is peace in the heart and soul. Peace is a result of the Sabbath!

You may be asking, "What does the Sabbath day have to do with peace?" Sabbath is a period of rest from everyday chores and busyness.

Exodus 20:8–10 *⁸ "Remember the Sabbath day by keeping it holy. ⁹ Six days you shall labor and do all your work, ¹⁰ but the seventh day is a Sabbath to the LORD your God. On it you shall not do any work, neither you, nor your son or daughter, nor your manservant or maidservant, nor your animals, nor the alien within your gates.*

When we partake of this quiet rest, we find inner peace and the strength to have peace with others, our environments, and with God.

Originally the seventh day of the week was set apart as the Sabbath. Now we observe the first day of the week. But the day that we observe the Sabbath really doesn't matter. What matters is that we keep it holy. It is a commanded blessing from the Lord given for our own good. Its purpose cannot be changed, except by Jesus Christ, for He is the Lord of the Sabbath.

Mark 2:27-28 *²⁷ Sabbath was made for man, and not man for the Sabbath. ²⁸ So the Son of Man is Lord even of the Sabbath [and He has authority over it]."*

The Hebrew word for Sabbath is shabbath, which means "to rest from labor". It was introduced in Genesis 2:2 when God Himself rested on the seventh day. He is and always has been our example, as manifested in Jesus. Again, the Sabbath was made for man as a day of rest, relaxation, and refreshing of the body and soul. In the Torah, or the Mosaic Law, there were stringent rules related to its observance. But the Jews used it to put people's lives in bondage by the same blessing that God had given them. But thank Jesus!

Although many of us do not think of it as such, the Sabbath is a necessary part of our health and well-being, physically, emotionally, and spiritually. Many of us wither and faint in the hustle and bustle of our lives. We have sudden heart attacks, strokes, and other health issues. We identify them as health issues rather than spiritual ones. But can we really be sure?

Listen, even the devil has a sabbath. It is a secret meeting of his followers to worship him, and it is characterized by orgies, parties, and services to ignite frenzied emotional behavior. This is their distorted version of the Sabbath of God. Always the counterfeit! But we need not worry.

Psalm 119:165 *Those who love Your law have great peace; Nothing makes them stumble.*

Leviticus 26:2-7 *² You shall keep My Sabbaths and have reverence for My sanctuary. I am the Lord. ³ If you walk in My statutes and keep My commandments and [obediently] do them, ⁴ then I will give you rain in its season, and the land will yield her produce and the trees of the field bear their fruit. ⁵ And your threshing season will last until grape gathering and the grape gathering [time] will last until planting, and you will eat your bread and be filled and live securely in your land. ⁶ I will also grant peace in the land, so that you may lie down and there will be no one to make you afraid. I will also eliminate harmful animals from the land, and no sword will pass through your land. ⁷ And you will chase your enemies, and they will fall before you by the sword.*

Loving God's law means we obey it; and obedience leads to peace. In fact, obedience is vital to peace. You can have no peace without it! Obedience is the fruit of righteousness. And oh, so much fruit it bears!

Isaiah 32:17-20 *[17] And the effect of righteousness will be peace, And the result of righteousness will be quietness and confident trust forever. [18] Then my people will live in a peaceful surrounding, And in secure dwellings and in undisturbed resting places.*

The blessings are in the obedience and obedience leads to peace.

Proverbs 16:7 *When a man's ways are pleasing to the LORD, he makes even his enemies live at peace with him.*

But the Word says Jesus did not come to make peace. Oh my! What does this mean for us?

Matthew 10:34-37 [34] *"Do not think that I have come to bring peace on the earth; I have not come to bring peace, but a sword [of division between belief and unbelief]. [35] For I have come to set a man against his father, and a daughter against her mother, and a daughter-in-law against her mother-in-law; [36] and a man's enemies will be the members of his [own] household [when one believes, and another does not]. [37] "He who loves father or mother more than Me is not worthy of Me; and he who loves son or daughter more than Me is not worthy of Me.*

The Message Bible [34-37] *"Don't think I've come to make life cozy. I've come to cut—make a sharp knife-cut between son and father, daughter and mother, bride and mother-in-law—cut through these cozy* *domestic arrangements and free you for God. Well-meaning family members can be your worst enemies. If you prefer father or mother over me, you don't deserve me. If you prefer son or daughter over me, you don't deserve me.*

Jesus came to divide the believers from the unbelievers. If that meant starting conflict between relatives, He was willing to do just that. Many times, we don't want to rock the boat, or disturb the peace, in our families. But that's just what Jesus came to do. It is my wholehearted belief that we must follow Jesus regardless of who does not want to come with us. This can be a difficult choice, but it is a necessary one.

Jesus is peace! But He knew that His Words would cause division and discord.

Hebrews 4:12 *[12] For the word of God is living and active and full of power [making it operative, energizing, and effective]. It is sharper than any two-edged sword, penetrating as far as the division of the soul and spirit [the completeness of a person], and of both joints and marrow [the deepest parts of our nature], exposing and judging the very thoughts and intentions of the heart.*

But He also left us with His peace!

John 14:26-28 *[26] But the Helper (Comforter, Advocate, Intercessor—Counselor, Strengthener, Standby), the Holy Spirit, whom the Father will send in My name [in My place, to represent Me and act on My behalf], He will teach you all things. And He will help you remember* *everything that I have told you. ²⁷ Peace I leave with you; My [perfect] peace I give to you; not as the world gives do I give to you. Do not let your heart be troubled, nor let it be afraid. [Let My perfect peace calm you in every circumstance and give you courage and strength for every challenge.] ²⁸ You heard Me tell you, 'I am going away, and I am coming back to you.' If you [really] loved Me, you would have rejoiced, because I am going [back] to the Father, for the Father is greater than I.*

What's the difference between God's peace and the world's peace? God's peace brings rest. The world's peace is temporary and leaves us hopeless and empty.

The Message Bible ²⁷" *I'm leaving you well and whole. That's my parting gift to you. Peace. I don't leave you the way you're used to being left—feeling abandoned, bereft. So don't be upset. Don't be distraught.*

There will always be things and people that Satan will use to come against us, even in the Name of the Lord; but Jesus left His Spirit to comfort us in those times of trouble. So never fret. God is still on the side of the righteous!

Psalm 37:11 *¹⁰ For yet a little while and the wicked one will be gone [forever]; Though you look carefully where he used to be, he will not be [found]. ¹¹ But the humble will [at last] inherit the land And will delight themselves in abundant prosperity and peace.*

And Ezekiel said the wicked will seek peace but will find none.

If we refuse to accept responsibility for our sin, then this does not apply. This is for the innocent who are being persecuted for the Lord's sake. The meek, the humble, and the peacemakers will inherit the earth!!! And those who keep the peace will be blessed.

Matthew 5:9 *Blessed are the peacemakers, for they will be called sons of God.*

The Message Bible *"You're blessed when you can show people how to cooperate instead of compete or fight. That's when you discover who you really are, and your place in God's family.*

When we have the fruit of peace, that Sabbath rest fruit, we can be peacemakers!

Psalm 34:13-15 *¹³ Keep your tongue from evil And your lips from speaking deceit. ¹⁴ Turn away from evil and do good; Seek peace and pursue it. ¹⁵ The eyes of the Lord are toward the righteous [those with moral courage and spiritual integrity] And His ears are open to their cry.*

This will keep you in peace, along with following the instructions in **Isaiah 26:3** *"You will keep in perfect and constant peace the one whose mind is steadfast [that is, committed and focused on You—in both inclination and character], Because he trusts and takes refuge in You [with hope and confident expectation].*

The Message - *People with their minds set on you, you keep completely whole, steady on their feet, because they keep at it and* *don't quit. Depend on God and keep at it because in the Lord God you have a sure thing.*

And when God gives you peace, it's ***all*** good. **Proverbs 14:30** A heart at peace gives life to the body.

For those who struggle with keeping their peace, walk in love, repent, forgive, praise your way to a state of joy, and meditate on this:

Psalm 91 *[1] He who dwells in the shelter of the Most High Will remain secure and rest in the shadow of the Almighty [whose power no enemy can withstand]. [2] I will say of the Lord, "He is my refuge and my fortress, My God, in whom I trust [with great confidence, and on whom I rely]!" [3] For He will save you from the trap of the fowler, And from the deadly pestilence. [4] He will cover you and completely protect you with His pinions, And under His wings you will find refuge; His faithfulness is a shield and a wall. [5] You will not be afraid of the terror of night, Nor of the arrow that flies by day, [6] Nor of the pestilence that stalks in darkness, Nor of the destruction (sudden death) that lays waste at noon. [7] A thousand may fall at your side And ten thousand at your right hand, But danger will not come near you. [8] You will only [be a spectator as you] look on with your eyes And witness the [divine] repayment of the wicked [as you watch safely from the shelter of the Most High]. [9] Because you have made the Lord, [who is] my refuge, Even the Most High, your dwelling place, [10] No evil will befall you, Nor will any plague come near your tent. [11] For He will command His angels in regard to you, To protect and defend and guard you in all your ways [of obedience and service]. [12] They will lift you up in their* *hands, So that you do not [even] strike your foot against a stone. ¹³ You will tread upon the lion and cobra; The young lion and the serpent you will trample underfoot. ¹⁴ "Because he set his love on Me, therefore I will save him; I will set him [securely] on high, because he knows My name [he confidently trusts and relies on Me, knowing I will never abandon him, no, never]. ¹⁵ "He will call upon Me, and I will answer him; I will be with him in trouble; I will rescue him and honor him. ¹⁶ "With a long life I will satisfy him And I will let him see My salvation."*

Let that promise escort you into your Sabbath rest with peace!

TIME TO MEDITATE ON IT

John 14:27 *Peace I leave with you; my peace I give you. I do not give to you as the world gives. Do not let your hearts be troubled and do not be afraid.*

Do you have a Sabbath Day according to God's commanded blessing? Do you have peace according to the promises of God? What steps can you take to increase the peace that you have with yourself, others, your environment, and God? You can do this! Just give it your best shot!

_____

_____

_____

_____

_____

_____

_____

_____

_____

_____

_____

_____

_____

Psalm 4:8 *I will lie down and sleep in peace, for you alone, O LORD, make me dwell in safety.*

CHAPTER FOUR
LONGSUFFERING: THE MERCIFUL FRUIT

In Matthew 17, the disciples were trying to cast a demon out of a man's son, but they were not having success. Jesus came and delivered him, but he was disappointed with the disciples, calling them faithless and perverse. They had no confidence in the power of Christ, so they had no power to withstand the enemy.

Matthew 17:14-17 *14 When they approached the crowd, a man came up to Jesus, kneeling before Him and saying, 15 "Lord, have mercy on my son, for he is a lunatic (moonstruck) and suffers terribly; for he often falls into the fire and often into the water. 16 And I brought him to Your disciples, and they were not able to heal him." 17 And Jesus answered, "You unbelieving and perverted generation, how long shall I be with you? How long shall I put up with you? Bring him here to Me."*

Another translation says in verse 17 Jesus asked, How long must I *suffer* with you? On another occasion, Peter decided that it was his job to tell Jesus what to do.

Mark 8:31-33 *³¹ And He began to teach them that the Son of Man must [of necessity] suffer many things and be rejected [as the Messiah] by the elders and the chief priests and the scribes, and must be put to death, and after three days rise [from death to life]. ³² He was stating the matter plainly [not holding anything back]. Then Peter took Him aside and began to reprimand Him. ³³ But turning around [with His back to Peter] and seeing His disciples, He rebuked Peter, saying, "Get behind Me, Satan; for your mind is not set on God's will or His values and purposes, but on what pleases man."*

Wow! What a correction! He was not mealy-mouthed in His response to Peter; but challenged him to reframe his thinking. It is always beneficial to have someone to help you identify those areas where the flesh nature continues to rise up. There are times that we don't realize the state that we are in, and we need someone to set us on fire, get us in the place of purification, deliverance, and healing. Iron sharpens iron and we need one another. We need someone to suffer long with us. But what did Jesus mean when He asked how long He must suffer or even that He must suffer many things.

Suffer means to feel and endure pain or distress or to sustain injury, disadvantage, or loss patiently and willingly. This suffering could even lead to death as it did for Jesus. In fact, He underwent the penalty of death willingly for us. Jesus also suffered in that He was rejected by the very people who should have been His first fruit. That pain runs deep! And some of us have treated Him that way at some periods in our lifetimes. But He is longsuffering…He suffers long with, and for, us! And we, like Him, must suffer through other's shortcomings and through our trials and persecution. In other words, just as Father God is patient with us and slow to anger, we must be with others, even sinners.

Paul spoke of it in I Corinthians 13:4 *Love endures with patience and serenity.* Colossians 1:11 tells us to suffer with joy: *[we pray that you may be] strengthened and invigorated with all power, according to His glorious might, to attain every kind of endurance and patience with joy.* This is not just about being willing to suffer for another person, but to do it with joy. Oh my! My toes are hurting right now! What about you? But we do this because we want God to do it for us.

Just as all of the fruit does, longsuffering produces Christlikeness. We need Holy spirit to carry this out in us due to our flesh nature as that nature cannot please God and doesn't even want to try. And although the flesh battles the Spirit of God, the Spirit must win in our lives by our agreement with Him! We must show progress! We are expected to grow in the grace needed to walk this out. And as He is patient with us, we must be patient with others, even ourselves. Patience is a form of suffering! It is enduring the uncomfortable, the ugly, and the unjust! But it produces fruit that will remain! Here's another example of His love exhibited by longsuffering.

Matthew 26:20-25, 36-50 [20] *When evening came, Jesus was reclining at the table with the twelve disciples.* [21] *And as they were eating, He said, "I assure you and most solemnly say to you that one of you will betray Me."* [22] *Being deeply grieved and extremely* *distressed, each one of them began to say to Him, "Surely not I, Lord?" ²³ Jesus answered, "He who has dipped his hand in the bowl with Me [as a pretense of friendship] will betray Me. ²⁴ The Son of Man is to go [to the cross], just as it is written [in Scripture] of Him; but woe (judgment is coming) to that man by whom the Son of Man is betrayed! It would have been good for that man if he had never been born." ²⁵ And Judas, the betrayer, said, "Surely it is not I, Rabbi?" Jesus said to him, "You have said it yourself."*

³⁶ Then Jesus came with them to a place called Gethsemane (olive-press), and He told His disciples, "Sit here while I go over there and pray." ³⁷ And taking with Him Peter and the two sons of Zebedee [James and John], He began to be grieved and greatly distressed. ³⁸ Then He said to them, "My soul is deeply grieved, so that I am almost dying of sorrow. Stay here and stay awake and keep watch with Me." ³⁹ And after going a little farther, He fell face down and prayed, saying, "My Father, if it is possible [that is, consistent with Your will], let this cup pass from Me; yet not as I will, but as You will." ⁴⁰ And He came to the disciples and found them sleeping, and said to Peter, "So, you men could not stay awake and keep watch with Me for one hour? ⁴¹ Keep actively watching and praying that you may not come into temptation; the spirit is willing, but the body is weak." ⁴² He went away a second time and prayed, saying, "My Father, if this cannot pass away unless I drink it, Your will be done." ⁴³ Again He came and found them sleeping, for their eyes were heavy. ⁴⁴ So, leaving them again, He went away and prayed for the third time, saying the same words once more. ⁴⁵ Then He returned to the disciples and said to them, "Are you still sleeping and resting? Listen, the hour [of My sacrifice] is at hand and the Son of Man is being betrayed into the hands of sinners [whose way and nature is to oppose God]. ⁴⁶ Get up, let us go. Look, My betrayer is near!" ⁴⁷ As Jesus was still speaking, Judas [Iscariot], one of the twelve [disciples], came up accompanied by a large crowd with swords and clubs, [who came as representatives] from the chief priests and elders of the people. ⁴⁸ Now the betrayer had given them a sign, saying, "Whomever I kiss, He is the one; seize Him." ⁴⁹ Immediately Judas went to Jesus and said, "Greetings (rejoice), Rabbi!" And he kissed Him [in a deliberate act of betrayal]. ⁵⁰ Jesus said to Judas, "Friend, do what you came for." Then they came and seized Jesus and arrested Him.

Here, Jesus exhibits longsuffering with His betrayer, Judas, and with his inner circle of friends, Peter, James, and John. Jesus could have killed him on the spot, but Jesus was willing to suffer long with him in order to allow him to carry out the Father's will. Then there was His disciples, who could not stay awake long enough to pray for Him in regard to the suffering that He was about to experience! This was tough for sure. Judas was His enemy, and His disciples did not appear to be concerned about Him! More rejection…but now from people that He had poured into for the past three years. He even still called Judas friend! What a Man! The other people cried "Hosanna" as He rode on the donkey, now they were yelling "Crucify Him!" Yet He still died for them.

Many of us may know how it feels when there has been betrayal by a loved one! But the only resolution is to forgive and walk in the very same loving, longsuffering position that Jesus took. We rarely want to do it, but longsuffering submits, endures, forgives! Peter denied Jesus three times, but Jesus said He would build His Church on Peter. We must show mercy just like Jesus!

In Matthew 18:23-35, a king wanted to collect his profits from his servants. A man, who owed him ten thousand talents (16 years' salary), was not able to pay. The king ordered that he and his wife and his children and all that he had be sold to repay the debt. The servant fell on his knees saying, 'Be patient with me (be longsuffering), and I will pay back everything.' The king took pity on him (was merciful) and canceled the debt and let him go. But verse 28 says But that same slave went out and found one of his fellow slaves who owed him a hundred denarii (one day's pay); and he seized him and began choking him, saying, 'Pay what you owe!'. His fellow servant fell to his knees and begged him, 'Be patient with me, and I will pay you back.' But he refused. Instead, he had the man thrown into prison until he could pay the debt. When the other servants saw what had happened, they were troubled and went to tell their master what had happened.

Matthew 18:32-35 *^{32} Then his master called him and said to him, 'You wicked and contemptible slave, I forgave all that [great] debt of yours because you begged me. ^{33} Should you not have had mercy on your fellow slave [who owed you little by comparison], as I had mercy on you?' ^{34} And in wrath his master turned him over to the torturers (jailers) until he paid all that he owed. ^{35} My heavenly Father will also* *do the same to [every one of] you, if each of you does not forgive his brother from your heart."*

The king showed his servant mercy, but the servant was unwilling to show mercy to his fellow servant. Many times, we are tempted to treat others in ways we would never want to be treated, especially not by God! This behavior is unacceptable to God. God shows us the mercy and longsuffering of the king. Because of His longsuffering, we are forgiven; so, we must forgive! That's why we pray, "Forgive us our debts **as** we forgive our debtors!" Otherwise, we are expecting something that we are not willing to give; so, we must pay our own debts in full…Pay it all!

Longsuffering requires acceptance of another's differences and beliefs, without a prejudice attitude. We should not even judge their conduct, character, or abilities. We are to show them respect for being who they are, looking for their good qualities rather than focusing on their faults, loving them as we want to be loved by Jesus. We must accept their shortcomings. I did not say we have to agree with what we see! But we do have to accept them as a creation of God.

Romans 15:1-7 *¹ Now we who are strong [in our convictions and faith] ought to [patiently] put up with the weaknesses of those who are not strong, and not just please ourselves. ² Let each one of us [make it a practice to] please his neighbor for his good, to build him up spiritually. ³ For even Christ did not please Himself; but as it is written [in Scripture], "THE REPROACHES OF THOSE WHO REPROACHED YOU (the Father) FELL ON ME (the Son)." ⁴ For whatever was written* *in earlier times was written for our instruction, so that through endurance and the encouragement of the Scriptures we might have hope and overflow with confidence in His promises. [5] Now may the God who gives endurance and who supplies encouragement grant that you be of the same mind with one another according to Christ Jesus, [6] so that with one accord you may with one voice glorify and praise and honor the God and Father of our Lord Jesus Christ. [7] Therefore, [continue to] accept and welcome one another, just as Christ has accepted and welcomed us to the glory of [our great] God.*

This is a sacrificial lifestyle. We must be willing to deny ourselves for the benefit of others. We must reach out with longsuffering to the sinner and saint if we want to please God. When it gets tough, God gives endurance and supplies encouragement. We must welcome into the kingdom all who will believe. Jesus did it; and so can we! This kind of patience makes us indivisible and therefore invincible!

Ecclesiastes 4:9-12 *[9] Two are better than one because they have a more satisfying return for their labor; [10] for if either of them falls, the one will lift up his companion. But woe to him who is alone when he falls and does not have another to lift him up. [11] Again, if two lie down together, then they keep warm; but how can one be warm alone? [12] And though one can overpower him who is alone, two can resist him. A cord of three strands is not quickly broken.*

We must be there for one another, with longsuffering acceptance, if we are to bear fruit and accomplish kingdom-building work of God! because of his longsuffering, we live! Because of His longsuffering, we have victory! Because of His longsuffering, we have power to suffer long in the face of the enemy! Because of His longsuffering, we live resurrected lives! These are the gifts that we received as a result of His longsuffering, and these are the gifts that we give others when we show them longsuffering. This is a good time to take a praise break for this merciful fruit of God!

TIME TO MEDITATE ON IT

Galatians 6:1 *Brothers, if anyone is caught in any sin, you who are spiritual [that is, you who are responsive to the guidance of the Spirit] are to restore such a person in a spirit of gentleness [not with a sense of superiority or self-righteousness], keeping a watchful eye on yourself, so that you are not tempted as well.*

How well are you at bearing the burdens or another? In what areas might you improve the fruit of longsuffering in your life? Need more lines? (smile)

_____
_____
_____
_____
_____
_____
_____
_____
_____
_____

Proverbs 15:18 *A hot-tempered man stirs up strife, But he who is slow to anger **and** patient calms disputes.*

Longsuffering: The Merciful Fruit

CHAPTER FIVE
GENTLENESS: THE SWEET FRUIT

Gentleness is the fifth of the nine fruits of the Spirit. It is the middle fruit…the one in the center of it all…hmm…like a yummy candy center (I digress)! Gentleness means to be kind. Some synonyms are sweet, innocent, inoffensive, tender, humane, polite, meek, mild, peaceful, merciful, submissive (not a bad attribute but has a bad rap), temperate; and manageable. I call it The Sweet Fruit because sweet means pleasing, agreeable, delightful, amiable, or friendly, kind or gracious, free from bitterness or sourness (know any bitter, sour people?), and easily managed.

Let's look at the meanings of a couple other synonyms. Innocent means blameless, guiltless, free from moral wrong, without sin, and pure. And inoffensive means causing no harm, trouble, or annoyance. Whew! Gentleness is a tall order, right?

When we walk in gentleness, we walk in love with kindness and humility and patience (longsuffering/mercy). In this way we can remain in peace with God, ourselves, and others. The act of gentleness includes the way we *feel* towards others. It indicates our humility toward God and others. It emanates from having a humble opinion of ourselves and it produces self-control when our emotions, don't want to line up. Sometimes, it feels like we are sheep among wolves (Matthew 10:16) and we actually are. But we can catch more flies with honey than acidy vinegar.

Proverbs 15:1-3 *¹A soft and gentle and thoughtful answer turns away wrath, But harsh and painful and careless words stir up anger. ² The tongue of the wise speaks knowledge that is pleasing and acceptable, But the [babbling] mouth of fools spouts folly. ³ The eyes of the LORD are in every place, Watching the evil and the good [in all their endeavors].*

We must be mindful how we talk to others. I know… some people are hard nuts to crack, even when you are gentle with them. But when we are speaking harsh words, we look foolish, just as foolish as they are acting. It's better to remove ourselves from these situations, at least temporarily, before we say something that we may regret. Words cannot be taken back or erased.

1 Peter 3:14-16 *¹⁴ But even if you should suffer for the sake of righteousness [though it is not certain that you will], you are still blessed [happy, to be admired and favored by God]. DO NOT BE AFRAID OF THEIR INTIMIDATING THREATS, NOR BE TROUBLED **or** DISTURBED [by their opposition]. ¹⁵ But in your hearts set Christ apart [as holy - acknowledging Him, giving Him first place in your lives] as Lord. Always be ready to give a [logical] defense to anyone who asks you to account for the hope and confident assurance [elicited by faith]* *that is within you, yet [do it] with gentleness and respect. ⁱ⁶ And see to it that your conscience is entirely clear, so that every time you are slandered **or** falsely accused, those who attack **or** disparage your good behavior in Christ will be shamed [by their own words].*

A gentle person is a peacemaker! It is what we call assertiveness. It's a win-win situation for all involved. And yes! We must have boundaries. We are not to be doormats. But gentleness characterizes us as Christians and gives legitimacy to what we say we believe.

Have you ever been in a store or restaurant after church and a customer, all decked out in their "church wear" and carrying their beautifully big Bible, yells at the worker arguing with them about "whatever"? That is a sad testimony for us as believers. And they *will* talk about us, and rightfully so. Many will even reject Christianity because they see no evidence of us being different than others. What good is it if we win our arguments, but lose their souls? God smiles when we operate with gentleness while others will not. Now that's a huge win!

Matthew 11:28-30 *²⁸ "Come to Me, all who are weary and heavily burdened [by religious rituals that provide no peace], and I will give you rest [refreshing your souls with salvation]. ²⁹ Take My yoke upon you and learn from Me [following Me as My disciple], for I am gentle and humble in heart, and YOU WILL FIND REST (renewal, blessed quiet) FOR YOUR SOULS. ³⁰ For My yoke is easy [to bear] and My burden is light."*

Sometimes we behave in inappropriate ways because we are stressed out, hurt, or abused. But here, Jesus promises a gentle rest for our souls when we face bitter or toxic people and situations. In the same manner, when we are gentle, others find rest for their souls. And when we are delivered into our gentle rest, we must not forget from whence we came. We should demonstrate to one another the same kindness Jesus has shown us!

A gentle spirit is one that is forgiving, quick to overlook sin, just as Jesus overlooks ours. Gentleness causes people to experience the love of Jesus. They see Jesus in us and experience the power of His forgiveness.

Colossians 3:12-13 *¹² So, as God's own chosen people, who are holy [set apart, sanctified for His purpose] and well-beloved [by God Himself], put on a heart of compassion, kindness, humility, gentleness, and patience [which has the power to endure whatever injustice or unpleasantness comes, with good temper]; ¹³ bearing graciously with one another, and willingly forgiving each other if one has a cause for complaint against another; just as the Lord has forgiven you, so should you forgive.*

Gentleness is an essential characteristic of any leader, 5-fold or not.

1 Timothy 3:2-3 *² Now an overseer must be blameless and beyond reproach, the husband of one wife, self-controlled, sensible, respectable, hospitable, able to teach, ³ not addicted to wine, not a bully nor quick-tempered and hot-headed, but gentle and considerate, free from the love of money [not greedy for wealth and* *its inherent power—financially ethical]. The leader must be holy, kind, disciplined, sober-minded, not easily offended, forgiving, free of strife, calm, compassionate, full of integrity, respectful of others, wise, and finally humble; yet strong when necessary. And he or she cannot be angry!*

Like Jesus, we should walk in humility while walking in authority. These two must be perfectly combined. To carry this out, we must walk in the spirit of gentleness, clothed in humility.

We must not quarrel but be gentle to all, able to teach, patient, in humility correcting those who are in opposition, if God perhaps will grant them repentance, so that they may know the truth (2 Tim 2:24-25).

Ephesians 4:1-3 *[1] So I, the prisoner for the Lord, appeal to you to live a life worthy of the calling to which you have been called [that is, to live a life that exhibits godly character, moral courage, personal integrity, and mature behavior—a life that expresses gratitude to God for your salvation], [2] with all humility [forsaking self-righteousness], and gentleness [maintaining self-control], with patience, bearing with one another in [unselfish] love. [3] Make every effort to keep the oneness of the Spirit in the bond of peace [each individual working together to make the whole successful].*

We do not belong to ourselves, so we must live as God desires. And God desires us to have a gentle Christlike personality.

We are gentle, not because of weakness or cowardice, but because of humility and inner strength!

How can we evaluate the amount of fruit we are bearing in this area? Well ask yourself, "How much gentleness do I exhibit when dealing with the undesirable circumstances in my life; especially when our religious beliefs, or ideas, are challenged? Can I maintain gentleness when others disagree with me and what may add up to being my religious, self-righteous feelings?"

1 Timothy 6: 11b-12 ...*pursue righteousness (not self-righteousness), Godliness, faith, love, endurance and gentleness (courtesy, politeness, respect). Fight the good fight of the faith. Take hold of the eternal life to which you were called when you made your good confession in the presence of many witnesses (others are watching).*

A gentle spirit is one of kindness and Godly love, not worldly lust. It is not an inward, selfish love. It's an outward expression of an inner relationship with God that is exhibited toward others (words without action mean nothing). The more love we give, the more love we receive. A gentle spirit is one of humility (not prideful and proud or boastful It is well-focused on things of God, not of the world.

1 John 2:15-16 *[15] Do not love the world [of sin that opposes God and His precepts], nor the things that are in the world. If anyone loves the world, the love of the Father is not in him. [16] For all that is in the world—the lust and sensual craving of the flesh and the lust and longing of the eyes and the boastful pride of life [pretentious* *confidence in one's resources or in the stability of earthly things]—these do not come from the Father, but are from the world.*

These sins, lust and pride, will cause us to lose sight of our purpose in the kingdom. They come with spirits of idolatry and gluttony. And they stem from covetousness and envy. Could we walk in the spirit of gentleness toward others with all of that going on? We couldn't! We would be too busy looking out for ourselves. But gentleness is unselfish. It is quiet; it is calm; it is sweet!

Gentle-men and Gentle-women reflect their Godly source, Jesus. Let this be true of all of us? Let's be as sweet as the water of the Well from which we spring.

God desires us to show the production of a gentle spirit! So, let's treat others with a gentle (sweet) Spirit just as the Lord treats us with gentleness (lovingkindness).

Matthew 5:5 *"Blessed [inwardly peaceful, spiritually secure, worthy of respect] are the gentle [the kind-hearted, the sweet-spirited, the self-controlled], for they will inherit the earth.*

The Message Bible "You're blessed when you're content with just who you are—no more, no less. That's the moment you find yourselves proud owners of everything that can't be bought.

Now that's worth me keeping my mouth closed when someone says or does something that I don't like! It's worth me taking a little opposition from people who mean me no good. And it's worth me loving them in the midst. It's worth giving up my rights in order to become a slave to Christ, receiving in return "everything that can't be bought." What about you?

TIME TO MEDITATE ON IT

Ephesians 4:32 *"Be kind and helpful to one another, tender-hearted [compassionate, understanding], forgiving one another [readily and freely], just as God in Christ also forgave you."*

In your life, are you growing in gentleness? Are you becoming more considerate of others? More attentive to their needs? More sensitive and soft with your responses? Less annoyed and irritated? More of a peacemaker? Take a moment and ask the Lord for forgiveness where you have been harsh and insensitive. Ask Him to help you be more sensitive, and to show you steps you can take this week to practice and grow in gentleness. Commit to Him to take these steps with His help.

_____

_____

_____

_____

_____

_____

_____

_____

_____

Goodness: The Ethical Fruit

Philippians 2:3 *Let nothing be done through strife or vainglory (excessive elation or pride over one's own achievements, abilities); but in lowliness of mind let each esteem other better than themselves.*

The Fruit of the Spirit

CHAPTER SIX
GOODNESS: THE ETHICAL FRUIT

Why would I call goodness the ethical fruit? Because goodness is all about integrity, wholeness, and right living! Goodness is moral excellence, virtue, kindness, and generosity. Synonyms include honesty, uprightness, and morality. Goodness signifies an overall quality of character and conduct that entitles the possessor to approval and esteem.

Sometimes, we can be so self-centered that we cannot imagine that anybody is good, but us! We don't trust anybody because we really think everybody else thinks like us! We all can be untrustworthy, at times. We often judge others by what we would do! So then, when God shows us His goodness, we don't show gratitude! We take Him for granted. We deal with Him like he is a piece of furniture, just sitting there waiting for us to *use* it. We must come into the knowledge that God is not a figment of our imagination! He is the True, Living, and Almighty God! He cares for you, and He is a Good Father!

In the Bible, goodness is not a passive quality. It requires an intentional choice to do and live right. This means we hate evil as much as we love righteousness. This is not intended to mean that we hate the evildoer; but we hate the act of evil. So, we resist it with all of our strength and authority through obtained through the grace given us by Jesus.

James 4:6-8 *⁶ But He gives us more and more grace [through the power of the Holy Spirit to defy sin and live an obedient life that reflects both our faith and our gratitude for our salvation]. Therefore, it says, "*GOD IS OPPOSED TO THE PROUD *and* HAUGHTY, BUT *[continually]* GIVES *[the gift of]* GRACE TO THE HUMBLE *[who turn away from self-righteousness]." ⁷ So submit to [the authority of] God. Resist the devil [stand firm against him] and he will flee from you. ⁸ Come close to God [with a contrite heart] and He will come close to you. Wash your hands, you sinners; and purify your [unfaithful] hearts, you double-minded [people].*

The fruit of goodness not only causes us to intentionally make decisions to do the right thing, but it also causes submission to God and resistance toward the devil. It stems from the integrity created while living in the other fruits. Goodness is also called kindness. It is impossible to be kind without submission to God's love.

Showing kindness means to favor someone, to have friendly feelings toward others, to show benevolence by doing good deeds and altruism, and to exhibit generosity, charity, sympathy, compassion, and tenderness toward others.

In Exodus 34, after Moses had thrown the first tablets at the Israelites for their idolatry, God told Moses to cut two more tablets and come to the top of Mount Sinai to receive the ten commandments for the second time. This is how God started His conversation with His friend!

Exodus 34:5-7a *⁵ Then the LORD descended in the cloud and stood there with Moses as he proclaimed the Name of the LORD. ⁶ Then the LORD passed by in front of him, and proclaimed, "The LORD, the LORD God, compassionate and gracious, slow to anger, and abounding in lovingkindness and truth (faithfulness); ⁷ keeping mercy and lovingkindness for thousands, forgiving iniquity and transgression and sin...*

This is a perfectly clear description of God's goodness. He totally cares about everything concerning us. He gives us the grace and ability to overcome our issues. He withholds His anger toward us so long that we sometimes think we have escaped consequences. This is because His love is everlasting through a thousand generations and His mercies are new every morning. But more than any of this He *forgives* our acts of unrighteous, morally repulsive, disobedience. He washes away our iniquities against others and our transgressions or violations against His commands. In other words, He allows our sins and detours from His known will without consuming us. Yes, the Lord is good, and His mercy endures forever forgiving all of our mess! And this is what He expects from each of us toward others.

God has shown His goodness more often than we can imagine. Here's another example.

2 Chronicles 32:24-26 *²⁴ In those days Hezekiah became terminally ill; and he prayed to the LORD, and He answered him and gave him a [miraculous] sign. ²⁵ But Hezekiah did nothing [for the LORD] in return for the benefit bestowed on him, because his heart had become proud; therefore God's wrath came on him and on Judah and Jerusalem. ²⁶ However, Hezekiah humbled his proud heart, both he and the inhabitants of Jerusalem, so that the wrath of the LORD did not come on them during the days of Hezekiah.*

Hezekiah had wandered off course. God extended His goodness and mercy. When we wander, it is important that we repent (turn away, never to return) and stay on course. In fact, God's goodness should provoke us to want to repent!

Romans 2:4 *⁴ Or do you have no regard for the wealth of His kindness and tolerance and patience [in withholding His wrath]? Are you [actually] unaware or ignorant [of the fact] that God's kindness leads you to repentance [that is, to change your inner self, your old way of thinking—seek His purpose for your life]?*

Many times, we want to tell of our own goodness (Proverbs 20:6) But it's always best to let someone else talk about how good you are!

Romans 15:14 (NASB) *And concerning you, my brothers and sisters, I myself also am convinced that you yourselves are full of goodness, filled with all knowledge and able also to admonish one another.*

We, the Church, should declare and decree God's goodness in our lives to others, especially those who do not know Him.

Goodness: The Ethical Fruit

Psalm 107:31 (KJV) *Oh that men would praise the Lord for his goodness, and for his wonderful works to the children of men!*

When we tell others what God has done for us, we are declaring His goodness. Tell others how far He has brought us so that they will know there is hope for themselves.

Ephesians 2:1-10 *[1] And you [He made alive when you] were [spiritually] dead and separated from Him because of your transgressions and sins, [2] in which you once walked. You were following the ways of this world [influenced by this present age], in accordance with the prince of the power of the air (Satan), the spirit who is now at work in the disobedient [the unbelieving, who fight against the purposes of God]. [3] Among these [unbelievers] we all once lived in the passions of our flesh [our behavior governed by the sinful self], indulging the desires of human nature [without the Holy Spirit] and [the impulses] of the [sinful] mind. We were, by nature, children [under the sentence] of [God's] wrath, just like the rest [of mankind]. [4] But God, being [so very] rich in mercy, because of His great and wonderful love with which He loved us, [5] even when we were [spiritually] dead and separated from Him because of our sins, He made us [spiritually] alive together with Christ (for by His grace—His undeserved favor and mercy—you have been saved from God's judgment). [6] And He raised us up together with Him [when we believed], and seated us with Him in the heavenly places, [because we are] in Christ Jesus, [7] [and He did this] so that in the ages to come He might [clearly] show the immeasurable and unsurpassed riches of His grace in [His] kindness toward us in Christ Jesus [by providing* *for our redemption]. ⁸ For it is by grace [God's remarkable compassion and favor drawing you to Christ] that you have been saved [actually delivered from judgment and given eternal life] through faith. And this [salvation] is not of yourselves [not through your own effort], but it is the [undeserved, gracious] gift of God; ⁹ not as a result of [your] works [nor your attempts to keep the Law], so that no one will [be able to] boast or take credit in any way [for his salvation]. ¹⁰ For we are His workmanship [His own master work, a work of art], created in Christ Jesus [reborn from above—spiritually transformed, renewed, ready to be used] for good works, which God prepared [for us] beforehand [taking paths which He set], so that we would walk in them [living the good life which He prearranged and made ready for us].*

When dealing with others, we must never forget from what God has delivered us. We were once sinners, but God showed His goodness to us in that He sent Jesus to die for our sins. He chose us and saved us by His grace. He drew us by His mercy. Then He seated us beside Himself in heavenly places and molded us into His own masterpieces. We are made new creatures by His love!

God's goodness has drawn us, and we can use kindness to draw others! Let's make Father proud by practicing ethically sound behavior, sharing the fruit of goodness with all those that we encounter. None of us like to be treated in an unkind manner. So, remember this when dealing with others. Stay focused on the love of God that has been shed abroad in your heart and shared in your life. Humbly submitting our feelings to Him will allow us to share the fruit of goodness that helps us treat others with the same kindness, grace, mercy, and love that has been afforded us by God. Remember, He loves you and He wants goodness to follow you all the days of your lives.

TIME TO MEDITATE ON IT

Jeremiah 31:3 *Yea, I have loved thee with an everlasting love: therefore with lovingkindness have I drawn thee.*

Have you had experiences when you did not receive kindness, or show kindness? How many times have you received undeserved kindness? Now, how often have you given undeserved kindness? What steps can you take to increase the fruit of goodness produced in your life?

_____
_____
_____
_____
_____
_____
_____
_____
_____
_____
_____
_____
_____

Romans 8:28 *And we know [with great confidence] that God [who is deeply concerned about us] causes all things to work together [as a plan] for good for those who love God, to those who are called according to His plan and purpose.*

The Fruit of the Spirit

CHAPTER SEVEN
FAITH: THE FRUIT OF AGREEMENT

Has God ever done anything impossible, or something miraculous, in your life? Something you knew couldn't have happened without his divine intervention? Think about it for a moment! What was it? How did He do it? Do you even know? Did you have to trust that it would work out? Well, faith is about making a choice, a decision, to trust God!!!

Hebrews 11:1 *Now faith is the assurance (title deed, confirmation) of things hoped for (divinely guaranteed), and the evidence of things not seen [the conviction of their reality—faith comprehends as fact what cannot be experienced by the physical senses].*

Yes, I know! This sounds familiar, even cliche. But how can one start a conversation about faith without expressing what the Bible says about it? Yes, I'm sure that you know by now, I'm one of them! So, let's break this down!

Faith is confidence or trust in a person or thing. It entails having an obligation of loyalty or faithfulness to a person, promise, or an allegiance. Faith is a confident belief in the truth, value, or trustworthiness of a person or thing, without tangible proof or visible evidence.

This is the kind of faith that we must have in God and His Son, Jesus Christ. We must believe the Word, that what He says is true. Remember, we are saved by grace through faith (Ephesians 2:8) so without faith we cannot even say that we are saved. This faith is what give us the ability to stay on the path of righteousness that God leads us on for His name's sake! Faith is a spiritual condition!

We must trust in the Lord with all of our hearts (Proverbs 3:5a) In order to have faith, we must not only believe that Jesus is Lord, but that it is beneficial to trust in Him.

Trust is the confidence in and reliance on the integrity, strength, ability, surety of a person or thing. It is confident expectation and hope in the certainty of a future payment.

Hebrews 11:6 *But without faith it is impossible to [walk with God and] please Him, for whoever comes [near] to God must [necessarily] believe that God exists and that He rewards those who [earnestly and diligently] seek Him.*

In Exodus, we know that Moses was charged with bringing God's chosen ones out of Israel. Pharoah kept promising to let them go, but he would change his mind. And after many disasters and plagues, Pharaoh finally let them go; only to come after them before they could get far. How many times has the devil left you for a season, only to return? Because of the Israelites fearful ways, God did not take them directly to the Promised Land through the Philistine territory. He knew they'd turn back to Egypt. So, He took them a safer but longer way (Exodus 13:17). Sometimes we wonder why God doesn't move quickly on our behalf. But He knows us well. He knows just what we can manage, and in His wisdom, He plans accordingly.

So, God led the people around by the desert road toward the Red Sea, leading them in a pillar of cloud by day and a pillar of fire by night. They thought they knew His plan. Then, in Exodus 14, God told Moses to turn back to camp by a sea so that Pharaoh would *think* they were confused and lost in the desert. The Israelites blamed Moses for leading them into harm's way although he was following God's direction by faith. God had a plan. He was going to make Pharaoh pursue them so that He could get the glory for their deliverance. See, God always has a plan, and He doesn't have to tell us what it is. We must have the faith and confidence to follow His leading. So, Pharaoh started his chase, boldly pursuing the Israelites, and overtaking them as they camped. Although Moses was upset at their reaction, he spoke with boldness that God would deliver them!

In verse 15, God ask why Moses was crying to Him and He told Moses to tell the Israelites to move on. That's what God says to us sometimes, right? Stop crying and get moving! Do what I am telling you to do! When we agree, He gives us further instructions. It's on a need-to-know basis and that was all they needed to know.

Exodus 14:31 *When Israel saw the great power which the* LORD *had used against the Egyptians, they feared the* LORD *[with reverence and awe-filled respect], and they believed in the* LORD, *and in His servant Moses.*

Moses followed God's instructions by faith, not naturally seeing the end of the thing, and his prophecy of the Egyptians' demise was fulfilled while the Israelites were saved. The Israelites believed because they *saw* what God did to the Egyptians. So, they feared and trusted God and Moses. But **faith** is belief that is not based on what we can see, but on trust in God and what He says!

Faith is the result of hearing the Word taught!

Romans 10:14-17 *¹⁴ But how will people call on Him in whom they have not believed? And how will they believe in Him of whom they have not heard? And how will they hear without a preacher (messenger)? ¹⁵ And how will they preach unless they are commissioned and sent [for that purpose]? Just as it is written and forever remains written, "How beautiful are the feet of those who bring good news of good things!" ¹⁶ But they did not all pay attention to the good news [of salvation]; for Isaiah says, "Lord, who has believed our report?" ¹⁷ So faith comes from hearing [what is told], and what is heard comes by the [preaching of the] message concerning Christ.*

I heard a wise woman say that some people have information, but no knowledge. Knowledge requires information, but information is no good without knowledge and understanding. Knowledge of God's

Word is an essential element in faith and is sometimes spoken of as an equivalent to faith. However, the two are different. Knowledge is the incorporation of information with what is already known for a better understanding. In contrast, faith is agreement, which is an act of the will, with God's Word even though we very well may not understand. Agreement with the truth is of the Spirit of faith. And the ultimate ground on which our belief in this revealed truth rests is the authenticity of God.

James 2 tells us of three distinct types of faith. Dead or inactive faith produces no results. It is inoperative and ineffective. It cannot because James describes it as the faith of a selfish person who doesn't trust God, so there is no evidence or corresponding actions. This faith has information but no knowledge. Really, the Bible is just a story with no impact on one's life.

Then, there is the faith of demons. Oh yes…they believe, but they only obey because they fear God. They know and respect God, but they don't acknowledge His will. They have works but they are not the works of God. This is an intellectual faith. It is temporary and only kicks in when trouble comes, a move of God is felt, or the Lion of Judah roars.

Finally, there is that faith that works righteousness. It is a saving faith that activates angels and motivates God to work on our behalf. It allows us to hear God and rest on His promises. It allows us to believe the Word and go when all signs say, "NO!" or "STOP!" Saving faith believes the Word is the only truth, so everything else is a lie. It is not just a spoken faith, but it agrees with God. It is a great faith with actions that scream, "God *will* do it!" And the greater the faith, the greater the harvest of other fruit.

Faith comes from a renewed mind and a determined will, without which we cannot live saved.

Mark 16:16 *He who has believed [in Me] and has been baptized will be saved [from the penalty of God's wrath and judgment]; but he who has not believed will be condemned.*

Faith is about agreeing with God just because He is God, and we believe that His Word is true. If we do not believe that He means what He says, we will not believe that He is who He says He is. We may believe today, but not tomorrow. So then, we cannot expect anything from the Lord.

James 1:5-9 *⁵ If any of you lacks wisdom [to guide him through a decision or circumstance], he is to ask of [our benevolent] God, who gives to everyone generously and without rebuke or blame, and it will be given to him. ⁶ But he must ask [for wisdom] in faith, without doubting [God's willingness to help], for the one who doubts is like a billowing surge of the sea that is blown about and tossed by the wind. ⁷ For such a person ought not to think or expect that he will receive anything [at all] from the Lord, ⁸ being a double-minded man, unstable and restless in all his ways [in everything he thinks, feels, or decides].*

A wonderful thing about this passage is that it is a reminder that we can always go to God to ask for wisdom when we lack it. So, we can ask Him for wisdom on how we can build our faith because we want to receive from Him all that He has for us. We know that all good gifts come from the Lord. Remember, God is goodness, the fruit that leads to repentance? If we really understand and believe how good God is, then we should have no problem trusting or obeying Him.

2 Chronicles 32:24-26 *²⁴ In those days Hezekiah became terminally ill; and he prayed to the Lord, and He answered him and gave him a [miraculous] sign. ²⁵ But Hezekiah did nothing [for the Lord] in return for the benefit bestowed on him, because his heart had become proud; therefore God's wrath came on him and on Judah and Jerusalem. ²⁶ However, Hezekiah humbled his proud heart, both he and the inhabitants of Jerusalem, so that the wrath of the Lord did not come on them during the days of Hezekiah.*

Here, when Hezekiah became ill, he prayed. And the Lord answered him by giving him a miraculous sign, even after he doubted God in even asking for a sign. This is the way of those who only believe God after they have seen signs and miracles. Remember when the apostles healed people after Jesus died? Many believed because of what they saw! Hezekiah did not agree with God or respond to His goodness. He thought he was in charge and did not trust God or His prophet. So, God's wrath was kindled against him, and because of him, against Judah and Jerusalem.

You see, our rejection of God through self-centered, rebellious, sinful, disobedient, and doubtful behavior will not only affect us, but also those around us. Thank God Hezekiah figured it out and repented, from his heart! God knew that his repentance was from a pure heart, rather than a prideful one. We must repent and turn away not to return, and stay on course, knowing that God is a good God who will forgive us if we are sincere! We must agree with God.

In John 21, John ends his book with a scene in which Jesus spoke to Peter. Jesus asked Peter the same question three times, "Do you love me?" The first two were asking if he loved Him as a brother; the last was about unconditional, agape love.

John 21:15 *So when they had finished breakfast, Jesus said to Simon Peter, "Simon, son of John, do you love Me more than these [others do—with total commitment and devotion]?" He said to Him, "Yes, Lord; You know that I [a]love You [with a deep, personal affection, as for a close friend]." Jesus said to him, "Feed My lambs."*

This must have been a difficult memory for Peter when he denied Jesus the same number of times. But instead, this helped to increase Peter's faith and confidence to become one of the early church's most fearless spokesmen. He did not run and decide he was not good enough. You see, *faith* produces confidence!

The devil will wear you out if you don't have faith in God! God does not expect us to have to see signs in order to believe. He expects us to have the faith to cast out demons and draw the unbeliever to the Lord!

Faith: The Fruit of Agreement

Proverbs 3:5-6 *⁵ Trust in and rely confidently on the LORD with all your heart And do not rely on your own insight or understanding. ⁶ [a]In all your ways know and acknowledge and recognize Him, And He will make your paths straight and smooth [removing obstacles that block your way].*

You don't have to understand how it works. Just do it! Just trust God! Can you believe what God says without seeing it? Do you want a *now* answer? Then, you must have *now* faith! We must believe what God says without seeing it if we want a *now* answer! Don't be like some of the Israelites, complaining and whining and lacking trust, because things are not going as you had hoped. With God, all things are possible...*if we would only believe!*

Before I talk about examples of great faith, let me leave you with this. Jesus encouraged Peter when he asked about His power to curse the fig tree. He needed more wisdom, so he asked, and Jesus answered.

Mark 11:22-24 *²² Jesus replied, "Have faith in God [constantly]. ²³ I assure you and most solemnly say to you, whoever says to this mountain, 'Be lifted up and thrown into the sea!' and [l]does not doubt in his heart [in God's unlimited power], but believes that what he says is going to take place, it will be done for him [in accordance with God's will]. ²⁴ For this reason I am telling you, whatever things you ask for in prayer [in accordance with God's will], believe [with confident trust] that you have received them, and they will be given to you.*

Just say words that agree with God! When we agree with God by having faith and by believing what He says, He releases our God-given desires to us!

Don't you want to be free from the lies of the enemy? Don't you want to see others delivered? Don't you want to see miracles, signs, and wonders? Then let's step up to the plate and trust Him with *all* our hearts?

TIME TO MEDITATE ON IT

Matthew 17:20 *He answered, "Because of your little faith [your lack of trust and confidence in the power of God]; for I assure you and most solemnly say to you, if you have [living] faith the size of a mustard seed, you will say to this mountain, 'Move from here to there,' and [if it is God's will] it will move; and nothing will be impossible for you.*

In what areas do you struggle with doubt? Which thoughts can you change in regard to trusting God? What actions can take today that will increase your faith?

_____
_____
_____
_____
_____
_____
_____
_____
_____
_____
_____
_____

Psalm 27:1 *The Lord is my light and my salvation— Whom shall I fear? The Lord is the refuge and fortress of my life— Whom shall I dread?*

Faith: The Fruit of Agreement

CHAPTER EIGHT
FAITH WALKERS

Hebrews 4:1 also tells us that there is a supernatural rest for us when we live by faith!

¹ Therefore, while the promise of entering His rest still remains and is freely offered today, let us fear, in case any one of you may seem to come short of reaching it or think he has come too late.

There is a maturity that comes with living by faith. When we refuse to live by faith, we do not grow, and we re-crucify Christ! But He came that we might have life, and that more abundantly! I want *all* that Jesus came, died, and rose for me to have!

Hebrews 4:2 goes on to tell us why people do not see results in their lives.

² For indeed we have had the good news [of salvation] preached to us, just as the Israelites also [when the good news of the promised land came to them]; but the message they heard did not benefit them, because it was not united with faith [in God] by those who heard.

We are told it is because, when we hear God's promises, we do not operate in faith to receive them. This means we are likely living in fear and unbelief, which opposes faith. We can have hope without faith. It's like having good ambitions and dreams, but no actions. So, it's fruitless! We must mix God's promises, for every area of our lives, with faith. Faith without works, or believing without actions, is dead, right?

Because of the way we have been socialized and because of some people's pride and need to control, we have learned to remain dependent on others and their faith far beyond the adolescent stage of development. In fact, the main task of a preschooler is to begin to learn to be independent. By the end of adolescence, this pursuit should be pretty well established. We should be looking toward growing into intimacy in our relationships. Psychoanalysts are speaking of intimacy within a male/female relationship. But, as Christian believers, we should know that before we seek intimacy with another person, we must seek an intimacy that can only be truly satisfied by Jesus Christ. He fills all of our voids; those that *no one* else can fill. But if we remain dependent on other people, we cannot and will not experience the intimacy or the security that we seek. We must learn to rely wholly on Jesus. This is faith!

2 Corinthians 1:20 *For all the promises of God in him are yea, and in him Amen, unto the glory of God by us.*

Paul is telling us that God's promises cannot be broken! They are 'Yes' and 'Amen'; but we must believe them to be true or they will not be experienced in our lives!

Let's review Hebrews 11. After the brief definition of faith, the writer begins to talk about the Faith Walkers! I want to point out just a few.

In the story of Cain and Abel (Genesis 4:1-16). Cain killed Abel entirely due to jealousy. In verse 4, it was written that Abel brought a better sacrifice to God than Cain. It was what he *believed*, not what he *brought*, that made the difference. God noticed this and approved Abel's offering as righteous. How often have you brought an offering to God with no faith attached to it? Well, here you see how God really feels about that offering. Faith will make you give your *best* offering, your *faith* offering…and *that kind of faith* pleases God!

Hebrews 11:6 *⁶ But without faith it is impossible to [walk with God and] please Him, for whoever comes [near] to God must [necessarily] believe that God exists and that He rewards those who [earnestly and diligently] seek Him.*

Why? Because anyone who wants to approach God must believe that He is alive and well, *and* that He cares enough to respond to us when we seek Him. God is faithful and true! He is even faithful when we are faithless! I am so glad to know that He will *never* leave, forsake, or fail us! If we know this, we can hold on to this truth no matter what we face.

Then there's Noah who built an ark for a flood in a dry season. To others, he looked insane. But he was following God's instructions. His instructions don't make sense to unbelievers. They rarely make sense to us! But Noah moved forward in faith.

Hebrews 11:7 *⁷ By faith [with confidence in God and His word] Noah, being warned by God about events not yet seen, in reverence prepared an ark for the salvation of his family. By this [act of obedience] he condemned the world and became an heir of the righteousness which comes by faith.*

Noah was warned about something he couldn't see, yet he acted in obedience on what he was told. The people thought he was crazy. But the result? His entire family was saved. Do you have family members that need to be saved? Obey God even when it seems insane, when it makes no *natural* sense! As a result of his crazy faith, Noah became intimate with God. And just as Noah's obedience clearly showed the distinction between believing God and being a faithless unbeliever, so should ours.

Abraham did the same, obeying God without knowing why he had to do it or what his outcome would be.

Hebrews 11:8-10 *⁸ By faith Abraham, when he was called [by God], obeyed by going to a place which he was to receive as an inheritance; and he went, not knowing where he was going. ⁹ By faith he lived as a foreigner in the promised land, as in a strange land, living in tents [as nomads] with Isaac and Jacob, who were fellow heirs of the same promise. ¹⁰ For he was [waiting expectantly and confidently] looking* *forward to the city which has foundations, [an eternal, heavenly city] whose architect and builder is God.*

With crazy faith, Abraham said yes to God's call to travel to a place that he had never been. When he left his family, he had no idea what could happen on the way to where he was going. When he arrived in the place that God sent him, he received a promise that the land would belong to his descendants. Along his travels, he experienced a famine that sent him to Egypt, told lies to survive, traveled through foreign lands, experienced wars, and rescued his nephew, Lot. But he *also* witnessed God's provision in and protection over he and his family. Abraham did this by keeping his eye on God's promise and he left his descendants to complete the journey into the promised land and lead us all into the blessings of God (Genesis 11-14).

And we can't leave out Sarah, Abraham's wife. In her old age, her faith was necessary for Abraham to see God's promise fulfilled. No, I didn't forget about Ishmael. He had a promise as well. But Isaac was called "the child of promise" because the promise was made to Abraham and Sarah.

Hebrews 11:11-12 *¹¹ By faith even Sarah herself received the ability to conceive [a child], even [when she was long] past the normal age for it, because she considered Him who had given her the promise to be reliable and true [to His word]. ¹² So from one man, though he was [physically] as good as dead, were born as many descendants AS THE STARS OF HEAVEN IN NUMBER, AND INNUMERABLE AS THE SAND ON THE SEASHORE.*

These faith walkers died, fully believing for the manifestation of what God had promised them! They had no evidence that it would happen other than their faith in God. They were not looking for *instant gratification*, but for promises they would not likely see fulfilled in their day. They looked to Jesus, the Author and Finisher of their faith! In this, God could be proud to call them His own.

But there is more on Abraham.

Hebrews 11:17-22 *17 By faith Abraham, when he was tested [that is, as the testing of his faith was still in progress], offered up Isaac, and he who had received the promises [of God] was ready to sacrifice his only son [of promise]; 18 to whom it was said, "THROUGH ISAAC YOUR DESCENDANTS SHALL BE CALLED." 19 For he considered [it reasonable to believe] that God was able to raise Isaac even from among the dead. [Indeed, in the sense that he was prepared to sacrifice Isaac in obedience to God] Abraham did receive him back [from the dead] figuratively speaking. 20 By faith Isaac blessed Jacob and Esau [believing what God revealed to him], even regarding things to come. 21 By faith Jacob, as he was dying, blessed each of the sons of Joseph, and bowed in worship, leaning on the top of his staff. 22 By faith Joseph, when he was dying, referred to [the promise of God for] the exodus of the sons of Israel [from Egypt], and gave instructions concerning [the burial of] his bones [in the land of the promise].*

Again, acting in faith, Abraham would agree to return God's promised and his only son, Isaac, back to his Creator even after he had already been told that his many descendants would come from Isaac. I'm guessing that Abraham figured, if God wanted to, he could change this course of action or even resurrect Isaac from the dead. As he initiated God's command, God delivered Isaac back to Abraham. Abraham got the opportunity to see just how great his trust in God was. When we are tested in any way, let it be our opportunity to see how deeply we trust God's plans for our lives.

Then there was Moses. Notice, his parents had faith when he was born or there would be no story to tell about Moses' faith.

Hebrews 11:23-29 *²³ By faith Moses, after his birth, was hidden for three months by his parents, because they saw he was a beautiful **and** divinely favored child; and they were not afraid of the king's (Pharaoh's) decree. ²⁴ By faith Moses, when he had grown up, refused to be called the son of Pharaoh's daughter, ²⁵ because he preferred to endure the hardship of the people of God rather than to enjoy the passing pleasures of sin. ²⁶ He considered the reproach of the Christ [that is, the rebuke he would suffer for his faithful obedience to God] to be greater wealth than all the treasures of Egypt; for he looked ahead to the reward [promised by God]. ²⁷ By faith he left Egypt, being unafraid of the wrath of the king; for he endured [steadfastly], as seeing Him who is unseen. ²⁸ By faith he kept the Passover and the sprinkling of the blood [on the doorposts], so that the destroyer of the firstborn would not touch them (the firstborn of Israel). ²⁹ By faith the people [of Israel] crossed the Red Sea as though they were passing through dry land; but when the Egyptians attempted it they were drowned.*

When Moses found out who he really was, he refused to continue to accept the 'rights' that he had possessed because he had been raised as the son of an Egyptian woman. He chose to be ostracized by those who raised him because he believed there would be a greater reward than what he had possessed. He chose to participate in the hard life with his people, God's chosen, rather than the easy life of luxury and sin with their persecutors. And he was willing to face the wrath of the king in the process.

Can you imagine living in an environment where everything you could ever want was available to you, only to give it up to live like a slave? Unthinkable for most! But due to his character, Moses gave up what he could have valued most.

Based on a faith he did not yet understand, he left Egypt and kept the Passover Feast, sprinkling the Passover blood on each house so that the lives of the Hebrew firstborn would be saved. He did not realize, at the time, that he was putting himself in position to be used mightily by God. Again, God doesn't have to tell us His plan. We just have to follow His leading! And to top it off, God had a plan to harden Pharoah's heart against the very thing He was telling Moses to do! Wow! Moses must have been frustrated and baffled, at times. But his faith caused him to push forward in the middle of Pharoah's persecution so that he could be a blessing to God's people.

But now the Hebrew people were also being punished for the words God was speaking through Moses. And now, he had to deal with their persecution as well as Pharoah's (sounds like a Jesus-type to me). We don't like persecution, but I believe that we all need a Pharaoh at times, to get us to our wealthy place. God's plan would ultimately bless His people and destroy their enemies. Remember, when they left Egypt, the Hebrews had the wealth of the enemy. And God parted the Red Sea to deliver them; then used that same sea to destroy their enemy; never to be seen again!

Then the writer noted that there were so many more,

Hebrews 11:30-38 *³⁰ By faith the walls of Jericho fell down after they had been encircled for seven days [by Joshua and the sons of Israel]. ³¹ By faith Rahab the prostitute was not destroyed along with those who were disobedient, because she had welcomed the spies [sent by the sons of Israel] in peace. ³² And what more shall I say? For time will fail me if I tell of Gideon, Barak, Samson, Jephthah, of David and Samuel and the prophets, ³³ who by faith [that is, with an enduring trust in God and His promises] subdued kingdoms, administered justice, obtained promised blessings, closed the mouths of lions, ³⁴ extinguished the power of [raging] fire, escaped the edge of the sword, out of weakness were made strong, became mighty and unbeatable in battle, putting enemy forces to flight. ³⁵ Women received back their dead by resurrection; and others were tortured [to death], refusing to accept release [offered on the condition of denying their faith], so that they would be resurrected to a better life; ³⁶ and others experienced the trial of mocking and scourging [amid torture], and even chains and imprisonment. ³⁷ They were stoned [to death], they were sawn in two, they were lured with tempting offers [to renounce their faith], they were put to death by the sword; they went* *about wrapped in the skins of sheep and goats, utterly destitute, oppressed, cruelly treated* [38] *(people of whom the world was not worthy), wandering in deserts and mountains and [living in] caves and holes in the ground.*

Joshua, Rahab, Gideon, Barak, Samson, Jephthah, David, and Samuel. Then there were the prophets who were protected, blessed, and victorious while others were tortured, abused, stoned, sawed in half, homeless, friendless, and powerless. Yet in Hebrews 11:30-38, they refused to quit chasing the things of God. I call these *Faith Walking Grownups*! They matured in their faith and did mighty exploits for God! Don't you want to be named among them?!?

Hebrews 11:39-40 [39] *And all of these, though they gained [divine] approval through their faith, did not receive [the fulfillment of] what was promised,* [40] *because God had us in mind and had something better for us, so that they [these men and women of authentic faith] would not be made perfect [that is, completed in Him] apart from us.*

Not one of these people, even though their lives of faith were blameless in God's sight, got to see what was promised. God plans for us to rejoice together in our faith even though we have lived in totally different spaces of time than they.

But let me tell you about a New Testament faith walker, one about whom I really love to study.

Mark 5: 25-34 [5] *A woman [in the crowd] had [suffered from] a hemorrhage for twelve years,* [26] *and had endured much [suffering] at* *the hands of many physicians. She had spent all that she had and was not helped at all, but instead had become worse. [27] She had heard [reports] about Jesus, and she came up behind Him in the crowd and touched His outer robe. [28] For she thought, "If I just touch His clothing, I will get well." [29] Immediately her flow of blood was dried up; and she felt in her body [and knew without any doubt] that she was healed of her suffering. [30] Immediately Jesus, recognizing in Himself that power had gone out from Him, turned around in the crowd and asked, "Who touched My clothes?" [31] His disciples said to Him, "You see the crowd pressing in around You [from all sides], and You ask, 'Who touched Me?'" [32] Still He kept looking around to see the woman who had done it. [33] And the woman, though she was afraid and trembling, aware of what had happened to her, came and fell down before Him and told Him the whole truth. [34] Then He said to her, "Daughter, your faith [your personal trust and confidence in Me] has restored you to health; go in peace and be [permanently] healed from your suffering."*

This woman had been suffering with uncontrollable bleeding for twelve years. She did not know what to do about it. She had spent all of the money she had seen doctors who only caused more suffering. Maybe she had also asked family members for assistance and priests to pray for her. But no one was able to help her; she only became worse.

But this *certain* woman heard that there was a *Man* going around healing all that were sick. But could, or would, He possibly help her? After all, no one else had been able to help get her healing. There may have been a tinge of doubt. Maybe she had even begun to feel that no one even wanted to help her because they seemed to have stopped trying. Maybe she was at her wit's end and ready to give up! Has anyone ever felt this way?

Then on this fateful day, a man came running through the streets, who everyone knew had been possessed by devils. He was screaming that Jesus had cast out the demons and he was delivered (Mark 5:1-20). When she heard this, hope began to spring forth and she began to get a fresh belief that healing was yet possible. Then she saw this Man, Jesus, walking along the road and she felt that her moment of healing was as near as He was. It was either do or die!

But who would help her? She couldn't just walk up to Him and ask Him to pray for her. That would be against her customs; after all, she was bleeding. But she also knew that no one had been able to help her before, so why would that be different today! But she realized that, if she were going to get the healing she wanted, she would have to take a risk and trust that she would be okay. She thought, "I may not be able to meet Him, but if I could only touch the hem of His garment, the power that flows through Him will heal me!"

She didn't just think or say it, she came to *believe* it with her whole heart! She knew that if she let her fear paralyze her, this may be her last opportunity for healing. She had to gather all of the strength and courage she could, press her way through this crowd, crawling on the ground if necessary, so that she could touch this Jesus who had what she needed.

In she went, pushing and pressing through the crowd, getting yelled at and judged. Imagine the thoughts and fears she must have experienced as she drew near. Others wanted to be up front to see Him. But she finally made it! She touched His garment, and she was finally healed and free from suffering.

Immediately, Jesus realized some of His power had left and He turned, asking "Who touched Me?" "Oh, no!" She had been discovered and she was in trouble now! "I will not respond to that question. Maybe He won't notice me."

The disciples wondered what Jesus was talking about because many people in the crowd were touching Him, so they said no one particular person had touched Him. But Jesus recognized that this was no normal touch! It was different. It was special! Some touches were just to see if He was real. Some were just so they could say, "I touched Jesus!" But this touch pulled on His virtue, His anointing, His goodness! Someone truly believed that something was going to happen to and for them when they touched Him. And He acknowledged that touch! Jesus knew someone had touch Him! He had felt that touch! And He kept looking for that person.

Now the woman realized that she could no longer hide, and again, though trembling with fear, she fell at His feet and spoke up. She told Him her story. She told Him how she had suffered for twelve years and depended on man to help her. She told Him how she had spent all of her money on doctors, only to get worse. And she had done all of this because she did not know Him or know that He would help her.

But she now knew that she needed Him. So, she poured out her heart to Him! Jesus, being Who He is, comforted her fears and assured her that, because of her faith, healing was hers. And He told her to go *with* peace and remain free from her suffering! Her faith had made her whole!

Notice, Jesus was on his way to heal Jairus' daughter (Mark 5:20-24), but He stopped and took time out for this woman. Isn't it nice to know Jesus is aware of us when we turn to Him and press in! We have to understand that Jesus knows when we reach for Him in faith! He knows when we come to Him wholeheartedly and when we actually expect Him to move on our behalf, not in a half-hearted effort to manipulate God. If we do, He will not answer. He is not mocked! Many times, He tells us what we need to change and how to do it; but we manipulate what He said to make it comfortable for us, rather than just being obedient. God will respond favorably when we humble ourselves under His mighty hand of healing and restoration, allowing Him to heal us and restore us to the place He has reserved for us! But we've gotta have faith!

This woman did not have to do anything but believe and act on what she believed. She knew no one else could do it for her; she would have to be the one to touch Him! It seemed to be a simple thing, but it took determination and courage to act on it. No one could give her the courage; she had to draw on her inner strength and move toward the Healer! After all, she had been suffering alone for twelve years. She had no other options! No one could give her relief! She had seen and heard about others receiving healing, but their healing could not be transferred to her by osmosis! She had to go to Him for herself! She had to have a personal encounter with JESUS! She didn't believe that He would require her to do anything strange or to jump through hoops to be healed. She refused to just go through the motions, as we often do! She believed that Jesus was her help, and He would not disappoint her! And she exhibited the simple faith of a child that brought her huge results. She may have been afraid, but she was not distracted, deterred, or paralyzed by it. Her focused act of faith and courage brought her exactly what she needed. She had tunnel-vision on Jesus, and He healed her!

Just like this woman, it is the faith to press forward, in spite of difficulties, doubt, or fears, and to touch Jesus that assures that we too can be made whole! Isn't that good news!

We have heard about some of the best examples of faith that we could ever ask for.

Hebrews 12:1-3 *[1]Therefore, since we are surrounded by so great a cloud of [a]witnesses [who by faith have testified to the truth of God's absolute faithfulness], stripping off every unnecessary weight and the sin which so easily and cleverly entangles us, let us run with endurance and active persistence the race that is set before us, [2] [looking away from all that will distract us and] focusing our eyes on Jesus, who is the Author and Perfecter of faith [the first incentive for our belief and the One who brings our faith to maturity], who for the joy [of accomplishing the goal] set before Him endured the cross, [b]disregarding the shame, and sat down at the right hand* *of the throne of God [revealing His deity, His authority, and the completion of His work].* ³ *Just consider and meditate on Him who endured from sinners such bitter hostility against Himself [consider it all in comparison with your trials], so that you will not grow weary and lose heart.*

They are called witnesses who have experienced God's faithfulness, even in their darkest times. Therefore, we have no excuses. We see that we can overcome all of our obstacles and be free just as these faith walkers that have gone before you.

Romans 1:20 *For ever since the creation of the world His invisible attributes, His eternal power and divine nature, have been clearly seen, being understood through His workmanship [all His creation, the wonderful things that He has made], so that they [who fail to believe and trust in Him] are without excuse and without defense.*

Even if we say that we have not seen God's faithfulness, we have read about it in the Bible, or at least here. That means we'd better get on with it. We must strip ourselves of every weight and start running—and never quit! We must build our faith muscles and beat down our flesh nature. We must keep our eyes on *Jesus*, who both began and will finish His good work in us. Stay in the race. Study how Jesus did it. He knew His purpose because He had heard it from the Father. He stayed focused in the midst of criticism, beatdowns, scandalous lies, and the Cross. And now He sits in His place of honor, at the right hand of the Father, knowing that it was worth it all.

This is why we must study the Word and stay in His presence. It is so we can overcome as He did! When we find ourselves slacking in faith, read His story again, line by line, and meditate on all that He endured for our salvation and purpose-filled lives. His love and faithfulness that caused Him to lay His life down for us should motivate us to stay on track! He went through more than we ever will.

Faith is knowledge of *and* agreement with God! Your faith will make you whole! So, let's be faith walkers together! Let's agree with God and let's get double for our trouble!!!!!

TIME TO MEDITATE ON IT

Romans 10:17 *So faith comes from hearing [what is told], and what is heard comes by the [preaching of the] message concerning Christ.*

Are you a faith walker? Ask God to increase your faith to that of those discussed! And ask Holy Spirit to help you agree with God's plans for your life. Your faith will change lives!

_____
_____
_____
_____
_____
_____
_____
_____
_____
_____
_____
_____
_____
_____
_____

James 2:24 *You see that a man (believer) is justified by works and not by faith alone [that is, by acts of obedience a born-again believer reveals his faith].*

Faith Walkers

CHAPTER NINE
MEEKNESS: THE FRUIT OF HUMILITY

What do you think it means to actually be meek? Many equate meekness with *weakness*, or an attitude of allowing everyone to run over you because of fear. They believe meekness is walking around with a solemn demeanor and never laughing; thinking that you are worthless. This is not meekness. In fact, some of the strongest men who have ever lived have been meek. And they demonstrate meekness with joy, which is the very source of their strength. Are you meek? That may be tough to answer without a definition so let me provide one.

Meekness means to be humbly patient when provoked by others. It means to be easily managed, surrendering, and yielding control completely. Its means to be soft and pliable clay in the hands of God!

We cannot be rigid and meek at the same time! You know that place where we do not have to be accountable to anyone who does not agree with us. That mentality can sometimes be your greatest enemy to growth! What about that place where no one can tell you anything because you already know the answers? And those times when we say we agree while sitting in silent rebellion on the inside. To be clear, this is not meekness. We must be open to receive the Word's instructions and *correction.*

James 1:21 *Wherefore lay apart all filthiness and superfluity of naughtiness, and receive with meekness the engrafted word, which is able to save your souls.*

Now let me ask again. Are you meek? God consistently requires meekness throughout scripture. It is my opinion that, without it, we will not show the light and character of God when offended, misjudged, or even justly disciplined. Bible translations use various words for meekness including gentleness, kindness, mildness, modesty, patience, and even temperance. But they all make the same point. Stay humble in all situations so that we are able to exhibits Christlikeness, as with all of the other fruits. Let's review a few of these scriptures in the King James version and other translations of the Bible.

Galatians 6:1 *Brethren, if a man be overtaken in a fault, ye which are spiritual, restore such an one in the spirit of meekness; considering thyself, lest thou also be tempted.*

The Living Bible *Dear brothers, if a Christian is overcome by some sin, you who are godly should gently and humbly help him back onto the right path, remembering that next time it might be one of you who is in the wrong.*

Ephesians 4:1-3 *¹ So I, the prisoner for the Lord, appeal to you to live a life worthy of the calling to which you have been called [that is, to live a life that exhibits godly character, moral courage, personal integrity, and mature behavior—a life that expresses gratitude to God for your salvation], ² with all humility [forsaking self-righteousness], and gentleness [maintaining self-control], with patience, bearing with one another [a]in [unselfish] love. ³ Make every effort to keep the oneness of the Spirit in the bond of peace [each individual working together to make the whole successful].*

1 Timothy 6:11 *But thou, O man of God, flee these things; and follow after righteousness, godliness, faith, love, patience, meekness.*

Phillips *But you, the man of God, keep clear of such things. Set your heart not on riches, but on goodness, Christ-likeness, faith, love, patience and humility.*

2 Timothy 2:24-26 *²⁴ And the servant of the Lord must not strive; but be gentle unto all men, apt to teach, patient, ²⁵ In meekness instructing those that oppose themselves; if God peradventure will give them repentance to the acknowledging of the truth; ²⁶ And that they may recover themselves out of the snare of the devil, who are taken captive by him at his will.*

Phillips *²⁵ But you, the man of God, keep clear of such things. Set your heart not on riches, but on goodness, Christ-likeness, faith, love, patience and humility.*

Meekness: The Fruit of Humility

Matthew 11:29 *Take My yoke upon you and learn from Me [following Me as My disciple], for I am gentle and humble in heart, and YOU WILL FIND REST (renewal, blessed quiet) FOR YOUR SOULS.*

Humility is having a modest opinion or estimate of one's own importance or rank. It means lowliness, meekness, and submissiveness. It means to be humble, modest, and courteously respectful. Meekness is humility; and humility is lowliness of mind. This quality enables us to see God and others with appreciation and joy, recognizing their good qualities rather than searching for their faults. We have to be mindful of offense, resentment, or any other obstacle. God *expects* us to produce this fruit. It takes diligence in working out your soul salvation, paying attention to our thoughts and emotions. But God offers us rest for our souls.

Romans 12:3 *For by the grace [of God] given to me I say to everyone of you not to think more highly of himself [and of his importance and ability] than he ought to think; but to think so as to have sound judgment, as God has apportioned to each a degree of faith [and a purpose designed for service].*

Some people think more highly of themselves than they ought, and this lends to difficulty producing meekness. Some may be prideful because they know the Word; or their position in the church or the body of Christ; some because they belong to a large or famous church. But whatever the reason, pride is always very offensive to God. It also indicates that this person cannot see the kingdom as God sees it because they are totally focused on themselves.

When we properly assess ourselves, most of us can see that we have nothing to be proud of or to brag about. Whatever good that is in us comes directly from God. If we have received anything from Him, we should give Him glory, instead of glorying in ourselves as if we attained it on our own.

We must make a serious effort to work on our humility. Humility focuses on others! Very few people have this quality innately. Most of us have to battle the carnal tendency of self-exaltation, always talking about what we have accomplished and feeling that we are superior to others. Then there are those on the other end of the spectrum who always feel like or talk about how they are not good enough. They are dealing with low self-esteem. Pride and low self-esteem are equally self-focused, and each removes our reliance on God! Remember, the Bible warns us that pride comes before destruction (Prov 16:18)! Don't self-destruct because of a lack of correct focus!

There are many benefits to being meek. God made special promises those who practice meekness; Isa. 66:2).

Matthew 5:5 (KJV) *Blessed are the meek: for they shall inherit the earth.* *(NLV) Those who have no pride in their hearts are happy, because the earth will be given to them.*

Meekness: The Fruit of Humility

Isaiah 66:2 *"For all these things My hand has made, So all these things came into being [by and for Me]," declares the LORD. "But to this one I will look [graciously], To him who is humble and contrite in spirit, and who [reverently] trembles at My word and honors My commands.*

I spoke of faith in the last two chapters. Faith is having confidence in God while trusting and accepting His will. **True meekness is childlike, even slave-like, submission to God's will for your life!** A good working definition of biblical meekness is *strength under control*. It takes humility to have this kind of faith! But the reward for meekness, for humility, is greater than anything that we can attain, or the world can offer.

Philippians 2:3 *Let nothing be done through strife or vainglory; but in lowliness of mind let each esteem other better than themselves.*

Paul says we should not do anything through rivalry or excessive pride over one's own achievements and abilities; but in meekness we should esteem others better than ourselves. True meekness thinks of others first. We will not be perfectly meek, but we *should* make progress. If you have come to Jesus, you know that you are not actually lower than all others. So, we know He didn't mean that we should rate ourselves as inferior to other men. Paul was saying that we should see ourselves through a lens of humility. In order to resist pride, we have to examine ourselves regularly keeping in mind that all gifts come from the Lord. We have a great responsibility to the Lord. Disconnected from that

Vine, we are nothing and can do nothing. We must examine whether we are even using the gifts given for *His* glory or for our own.

Meekness is a state of mind that is teachable and pliable, not rigid and resistant! It is a state of mind that opens doors for God, and man, to honor you! God said He would esteem us!

James 4:10 *Humble yourselves [with an attitude of repentance and insignificance] in the presence of the Lord, and He will exalt you [He will lift you up, He will give you purpose].*

Now that's worth me monitoring my thoughts and actions and keeping my mouth closed when someone says or does something I don't like! It's worth me taking a little flak from people who mean me no good! And it's worth me loving them in the midst! It's worth giving up my rights in order to become a slave to Christ, receiving in return "everything that can't be bought"! What about you?

1 Peter 3:8-18 *⁸ Finally, all of you be like-minded [united in spirit], sympathetic, brotherly, kindhearted [courteous and compassionate toward each other as members of one household], and humble in spirit; ⁹ and never return evil for evil or insult for insult [avoid scolding, berating, and any kind of abuse], but on the contrary, give a blessing [pray for one another's well-being, contentment, and protection]; for you have been called for this very purpose, that you might inherit a blessing [from God that brings well-being, happiness, and protection]. ¹⁰ For, "THE ONE WHO WANTS TO ENJOY LIFE AND SEE GOOD DAYS [good—whether apparent or not], MUST KEEP HIS TONGUE FREE FROM EVIL AND HIS LIPS FROM SPEAKING GUILE (treachery, deceit).*

[11] *"HE MUST TURN AWAY FROM WICKEDNESS AND DO WHAT IS RIGHT. HE MUST SEARCH FOR PEACE [with God, with self, with others] AND PURSUE IT EAGERLY [actively—not merely desiring it].* *[12]* *"FOR THE EYES OF THE LORD ARE [looking favorably] UPON THE RIGHTEOUS (the upright), AND HIS EARS ARE ATTENTIVE TO THEIR PRAYER (eager to answer), BUT THE FACE OF THE LORD IS AGAINST THOSE WHO PRACTICE EVIL."*

The Message *[8-12]Summing up: Be agreeable, be sympathetic, be loving, be compassionate, be humble. That goes for all of you, no exceptions. No retaliation. No sharp-tongued sarcasm. Instead, bless—that's your job, to bless. You'll be a blessing and also get a blessing. Whoever wants to embrace life and see the day fill up with good, Here's what you do: Say nothing evil or hurtful; Snub evil and cultivate good; run after peace for all you're worth. God looks on all this with approval, listening and responding well to what he's asked; But he turns his back on those who do evil things.*

If it's good enough for Jesus, it's good enough for me! In these last days, we are going to need meekness more than ever. Our inheritance also speaks to the power and authority to overcome the enemy *in this day*.

So, let's grow in meekness and humility so we can obtain our inheritance of honor from God and expect victory!

TIME TO MEDITATE ON IT

Colossians 3:12 *Put on therefore, as the elect of God, holy and beloved, bowels of mercies, kindness, humbleness of mind, meekness, longsuffering;*

Take a moment and consider: Are you using the gifts and talents that God has given you? Are you giving God your best? Are you humble about those gifts? In what area(s) can you do better?

_____

_____

_____

_____

_____

_____

_____

_____

_____

_____

_____

_____

_____

_____

Meekness: The Fruit of Humility

Zephaniah 2:3 *Seek ye the LORD, all ye meek of the earth, which have wrought his judgment; seek righteousness, seek meekness: it may be ye shall be hid in the day of the LORD's anger.*

The Fruit of the Spirit

CHAPTER TEN
TEMPERANCE: THE FRUIT OF INSURANCE

Ephesians 4:1-3 *¹ So I, the prisoner for the Lord, appeal to you to live a life worthy of the calling to which you have been called [that is, to live a life that exhibits godly character, moral courage, personal integrity, and mature behavior—a life that expresses gratitude to God for your salvation], ² with all humility [forsaking self-righteousness], and gentleness [maintaining self-control], with patience, bearing with one another in [unselfish] love. ³ Make every effort to keep the oneness of the Spirit in the bond of peace [each individual working together to make the whole successful].*

I believe there is a reason that love is the first fruit mentioned. I don't believe we can live for Jesus without it. I also believe that there is a reason temperance is the last fruit mentioned. I believe it encompasses the others. The other fruit are like the filing for a great wrap; but they need something to hold all of those goodies together. And I truly believe that we cannot live a long, fruitful life without temperance!

Temperance is the habitual moderation in the indulgence of a natural appetite or passion. It is self-control, moderation, or self-restrain. Moderation is the avoidance of extremes or excesses. In order to be temperate, we must avoid excesses and find balance. Balance is a state of equilibrium or equal distribution of weight. It also means mental steadiness or emotional stability and a habit of calm behavior or judgment. When we bear the fruit of temperance, we are stable in all of our ways whether it is behavioral, emotional, or mental.

Proverbs 25:28 *Like a city that is broken down and without walls [leaving it unprotected] is a man no self-control over his spirit [and sets himself up for trouble].*

The Message [28] *a person without self-control is like a house with its doors and windows knocked out. That means, any storm can blow it down or blow it away!*

You've heard the phrase, "do all things in moderation". It has been preached over the pulpit and we thought it was a scripture that permitted us to do anything, good or bad, as long as we didn't *overdo* it? But knowledge and context are critical to the understanding of a thing, even temperance!

The phrase is actually "moderation in all things" and it was originated by Aristotle, the philosopher. He believed that we should find the perfect balance between extremes, a mean or middle ground so to speak between excess and lack in all areas, if we are to be happy. We should not approach *all* things (whether healthy or unhealthy) with moderation. Assuming it is alright to indulge in a moderate amount of a bad thing is considered faulty thinking.

When we are out of balance, longing for the right things too much or not enough, we make unhealthy decisions due to skewed thoughts and emotions that cause us to behave rashly out of fear. This will could put us in harm's way and detour our road to true happiness (good fortune or contentment). We will also find it quite difficult to discover true joy (great delight caused by something exceptionally satisfying) in Jesus. The sources of each of these are not the same. Joy comes internally from a relationship with the Lord Jesus. Happiness comes from external conditions and stimuli such as wealth, health, fulfilling activities, relationships, and independence.

So, how did this become accepted as scripture? Though there is no direct scripture matching Aristotle's concept, Paul expresses a similar thought in his description of a winning athlete.

1 Corinthians 9:25 *Now every athlete who [goes into training and] competes in the games is disciplined and exercises self-control in all things. They do it to win a crown that withers, but we [do it to receive] an imperishable [crown that cannot wither].*

Paul could be referring to Aristotle's concept. But it's more likely that he was steering us toward temperance in all things, or being in total self-control. So, the belief that we can do anything as long as we do it with moderation is not what was meant by either writer. This interpretation should not be embraced, especially in the body of Christ. Some things we can do a bit of, and others we must abstain from altogether! This is why I say we cannot live long without the fruit of temperance! We must study the Word to know the difference.

2 Peter 1:5-7 *⁵For this very reason, applying your diligence [to the divine promises, make every effort] in [exercising] your faith to, develop moral excellence (goodness), and in moral excellence, knowledge (insight, understanding), ⁶and in your knowledge, self-control (temperance), an in your self-control, steadfastness (long-suffering); and in your steadfastness, godliness; ⁷And in your godliness, brotherly affection (kindness); and to brotherly affection, [develop Christian] love [that is, learn to unselfishly seek the best for others and do things for their benefit (humility)].*

I love this scripture because it incorporates many of the fruit that we have reviewed. To be sure, we need temperance when it comes to ridding ourselves of the bad habits of which we are aware! We should examine ourselves so that we know what they are! We all have them!

What are those things you feel you cannot live without, even though God has said a resounding *"NO" to* them? Those are the things that cause a lack of control! They can steal your life spiritually, and maybe even physically! Why? In these areas, we are unprotected!

We must learn to be temperate in word and deed! 1 Timothy 3, Paul advocated for temperance of leaders and older adults. And he said in 1 Corinthians 9 that anyone who wants to win is temperate in all things!

God brings us to Himself so that we can learn to work out our own soul's salvation by utilizing self-control! We must work on those things that we think, feel, and will to do (things we feel are our right or that to which we believe we're entitled). These things can form addictions; yes, we can become addicted to anything! When we lack temperance, our lives become unmanageable. Here are a few examples:

- We can talk too much (tell someone's business, relate misinformation, or just tell too much of your own business) and someone hurts us!

    Proverbs 20:19 *He who goes about as a gossip reveals secrets; Therefore do not associate with a gossip [who talks freely or flatters].*

- We can eat or drink too much, overindulge in things, or commit idolatry!

    Philippians 3:18-19 *[18] For there are many, of whom I have often told you, and now tell you even with tears, who live as enemies of the cross of Christ [rejecting and opposing His way of salvation], [19] whose fate is destruction, whose god is **their** belly [their worldly appetite, their sensuality, their vanity], and **whose** glory is in their shame—who focus their mind on earthly and temporal things. [20] But [we are different, because] our citizenship is in heaven. And from there we eagerly await [the coming of] the Savior, the Lord Jesus Christ;*

Proverbs 23:2 *For you will put a knife to your throat If you are a man of **great** appetite.*

CEV *Don't go and stuff yourself! That would be just the same as cutting your throat.*

Proverbs 23:21 *For the heavy drinker and the glutton will come to poverty, And the drowsiness [of overindulgence] will clothe one with rags.*

1 Corinthians 6:9-10 *(NIV) ⁹do you not know that the wicked will not inherit the kingdom of God? Do not be deceived: neither the sexually immoral nor idolaters nor adulterers nor male prostitutes nor homosexual offenders ¹⁰nor thieves nor the greedy nor drunkards nor slanderers nor swindlers will inherit the kingdom of God.*

Oops! There goes the demise of that moderation theory.

- We can spend too aggressively and have no seed to sow or spend so much that we become homeless. We must steward our seed wisely if we are to rule with Jesus! We don't want to be lacking at a critical time like the foolish virgin!

  Luke 12:42 *The Lord said, "Who then is the faithful and wise steward [of the estate], whom his master will put in charge over his household, to give his servants their portion of food at the proper time?*

Temperance: The Fruit of Insurance

Matthew 25:1-13 *Then shall the kingdom of heaven be likened unto ten virgins, which took their lamps, and went forth to meet the bridegroom. [2] And five of them were wise, and five were foolish. [3] They that were foolish took their lamps, and took no oil with them: [4] But the wise took oil in their vessels with their lamps. [5] While the bridegroom tarried, they all slumbered and slept. [6] And at midnight there was a cry made, Behold, the bridegroom cometh; go ye out to meet him. [7] Then all those virgins arose, and trimmed their lamps. [8] And the foolish said unto the wise, Give us of your oil; for our lamps are gone out. [9] But the wise answered, saying, Not so; lest there be not enough for us and you: but go ye rather to them that sell, and buy for yourselves. [10] And while they went to buy, the bridegroom came; and they that were ready went in with him to the marriage: and the door was shut. [11] Afterward came also the other virgins, saying, Lord, Lord, open to us. [12] But he answered and said, Verily I say unto you, I know you not. [13] Watch therefore, for ye know neither the day nor the hour wherein the Son of man cometh.*

They were left behind with no place of rest; homeless and without the Lord!

- We can move too fast and lose our balance!

Hebrews 12:1-2 *[1] Wherefore seeing we also are compassed about with so great a cloud of witnesses, let us lay aside every weight, and the sin which doth so easily beset us, and let us* *run with patience the race that is set before us, ²Looking unto Jesus the author and finisher of our faith; who for the joy that was set before him endured the cross, despising the shame, and is set down at the right hand of the throne of God.*

Slow down! Rest! God will see to it that you reach your destination!

- We can seek too much attention and draw the attention from the wrong source. We really need control in this area. By the way, negative attention is <u>not</u> better than no attention at all! We only need God's attention.

PS 8:4-6 *⁴what is man that you are mindful of him, the son of man that you care for him? ⁵You made him a little lower than the heavenly beings and crowned him with glory and honor. ⁶You made him ruler over the works of your hands; you put everything under his feet:*

You are important to Him. When that's not enough, you will people please, and you will lose self-control!

Ephesians 6:5-7 (ESV) *⁵Bondservants, obey your earthly masters with fear and trembling, with a sincere heart, as you would Christ, ⁶not by the way of eye-service, as people-pleasers, but as bondservants of Christ, doing the will of God from the heart, ⁷rendering service with a good will as to the Lord and not to man,*

We are slaves to *no* man. However, we should serve others as if we are serving the Lord! Because we are!!!

- We can worry too much and lose gratitude for what God is doing, or even lose our minds!

Philippians 4:6-7 *⁶Do not be anxious or worried about anything, but in everything [every circumstance and situation] by prayer and petition with thanksgiving, continue to make your [specific] requests known to God. ⁷ And the peace of God [that peace which reassures the heart, that peace] which transcends all understanding, [that peace which] stands guard over your hearts and your minds in Christ Jesus [is yours].*

We must allow God's peace (that sabbath fruit) to guard our hearts and our minds through Christ!

- We can get too angry and lose our freedom!

Proverbs 19:19 *A hot-tempered man must pay the penalty; if you rescue him, you will have to do it again.*

Proverbs 29:11 *A fool gives full vent to his anger, but a wise man keeps himself under control.*

We must begin to take account of our uncontrollable behaviors and mindsets. We must abstain from those things that keep us from the fruit of temperance. Similarly, we can't afford to procrastinate or become complacent in our successes, resting on our laurels. There is so much more that God has for us if we will just buckle down, grow up, and obey him! We may not see it now. But Isaiah 55:8 reminds us that His thoughts are not our thoughts, and our ways are not His ways. We must trust in the Lord and not rely on our own interpretations of life. We must trust Him in every situation, knowing He's guiding our steps (Proverbs 3:5-6). So, we don't have to be in control of what's happening. We can trust that He knows. We are only responsible for allowing Him to lead us on a righteous pathway! Why? Because He cares for you!

Temperance is the greatest protection we can have against the enemy of our souls. It is the insurance that we need if we are to walk in the other fruits! And this is a no cost insurance. We attain it by submitting to the Lover of our souls; and by walking in love with those that He loves! When we submit to God, we are covered! Won't you give yourself fully to Him today?

Temperance: The Fruit of Insurance

TIME TO MEDITATE ON IT

1 Corinthians 9:25 *Now every athlete who [goes into training and] competes in the games is disciplined and exercises self-control in all things. They do it to win a crown that withers, but we [do it to receive] an imperishable [crown that cannot wither].*

What are those things you feel you cannot live without, even though God has said a resounding *"no" to* them? What are your bad habits...areas where you need to practice self-control?

_____
_____
_____
_____
_____
_____
_____
_____
_____
_____
_____
_____

1 Thessalonians 5:6 *So then let us not sleep [in spiritual indifference] as the rest [of the world does], but let us keep wide awake [alert and cautious] and let us be sober [self-controlled, calm, and wise].*

CHAPTER ELEVEN
OK, WHAT'S NEXT?

I know this may seem like an impossible task, producing all of this fruit. But as we surrender to the Father, He will produce in us what we could never, ever produce in ourselves. Yielding submits to pruning. Without pruning, there is no yielding.

John 15:1-3 *"I am the true Vine, and My Father is the vinedresser. ² Every branch in Me that does not bear fruit, He takes away; and every branch that continues to bear fruit, He [repeatedly] prunes, so that it will bear more fruit [even richer and finer fruit]. ³ You are already clean because of the word which I have given you [the teachings which I have discussed with you].*

Pruning removes any useless, unwanted attachments. It offers the opportunity for growth and maturity. When we resist or rebel against the pruning process, we displease God and, with that, there are always self-created consequences.

Isaiah 5:6 *"I will turn it into a wasteland; It will not be pruned or cultivated, But briars and thorns will come up. I will also command the clouds not to rain on it."*

The pruning process *cannot* be avoided if we want to produce the fruit of the Spirit! Pruning produces a great yield for a harvest of fruit. Though it can be painful in the moment, the fruit yielded will be the best fruit, God's fruit. The fruit will be utilized for our most useful ministry of His love to others.

Let me warn you...pruning is a lifelong occurrence. As long as we abide in the Vine, we will be pruned. I know we always want to avoid the tough part of growth, or at least for it to pass quickly. But we also know that avoidance of what is good for us is never good for us!

As we surrender to our pruning process, we begin to love like Jesus. We find a joy that we never thought we could experience. We attain an inner peace we don't really understand. We seem to endure the process with much more genuine patience as we practice longsuffering with ourselves and those around us. We experience the lovingkindness of the Lord, and we can share His with others.

We begin to recognize that it is only God's goodness that sustains us through the process. He makes us lie down in green pastures and restores our souls as He molds and shapes us into the vessels that are fit for His use. His faithfulness becomes a trait of our very own because we are building faith in Him so we can be converted ans transformed. Gentleness develops in us as we submit to His love and rest in His peace. And we begin to experience the temperance produced by practicing the other fruit. We begin to understand how God practices self-control in His dealings with us.

As we can see, the fruit of the Spirit is His fruit! It comes through us from Him. We are partakers of God's attributes and that in itself is a privilege! We must know that God wants us to be successfully fruitful! This is how we multiply His Kingdom. He says in Galatians 5:23, in this there is no law.

Galatians 5:24-26 *²⁴ And those who belong to Christ Jesus have crucified the sinful nature together with its passions and appetites. ²⁵ If we [claim to] live by the [Holy] Spirit, we must also walk by the Spirit [with personal integrity, godly character, and moral courage—our conduct empowered by the Holy Spirit]. ²⁶ We must not become conceited, challenging or provoking one another, envying one another.*

If you have taken the time to read this, I know that you are either already a believer in the Lord, or you really want to become one! The above verses explain that we have been saved from the sin nature that causes us not to produce fruit. We are not only saved through the Cross, but we are also working out our own soul salvation so that we are in position to be pruned to produce fruit. We are bringing the flesh nature into submission to God by aligning our hearts and minds with His Spirit. So, we walk in personal integrity (that is, as one who has been made whole, walking as one with Christ), Godly character, and moral courage (boldly declaring the Gospel of Jesus Christ). All of this is due to being connected to the Vine Who infused us with the grace, power, and ability to produce His fruit and mature into the likeness of Christ.

We will not walk in pride if we keep that fact in mind. It is HIS fruit! We are just carriers. As we acknowledge our own weaknesses from which God has delivered us, we will walk in the humility required to treat others as He would have us treat them, walking together as one Body, without division or competition. This is the will of God for our lives. He is waiting for a Bride that can take with Him into eternity.

Ephesians 5:25-27 *25 Husbands, love your wives [seek the highest good for her and surround her with a caring, unselfish love], just as Christ also loved the church and gave Himself up for her, 26 so that He might sanctify the church, having cleansed her by the washing of water with the word [of God], 27 so that [in turn] He might present the church to Himself in glorious splendor, without spot or wrinkle or any such thing; but that she would be holy [set apart for God] and blameless.*

I know this was written to earthly husbands. But they are just being told to replicate their treatment of their wives as Christ has treated His Bride, giving himself up totally for us, life and all! He gave up His reputation and position to save us from ourselves. He has loved us, given His blood for us, and sanctified and cleansed us by His Word. He has also empowered us to carry out His will in the earth. And He did all of this so that we can be a Bride that He might take home with Him…a holy Bride without spot or wrinkle!!!

Don't you want to be His beautiful Bride without scars and flaws in the sight of our Lord? Don't you want to be with someone Who will not point out your deficiencies, but only His love for you? Well, we can only find that in Jesus. He is the Truth, the Way, and the Life! And He is seated in heavenly places with the Father, interceding for us that we make it. He is on our side! Let's join forces with Him, shine His light through our fruit bearing, and give the world the opportunity to see the Savior!

Yes! You too can be shining – bearing fresh fruit! Even if you are already bearing fruit, there is more to come! I see you! But more importantly, Father God sees you! So, walk boldly, full of the fruit of His Spirit!

OK, What's Next?

About the Author

Doretha McBride is a native of Chicago, IL, the youngest of nine children, and an undistracted widow since April 2008. Doretha has experienced an arduous life journey but has pressed onward toward the things of God motivated by His Love and His Promise to "take good care of her." Because of her personal experience of transformation and the resulting wisdom imparted into her life, her desire has been to help others experience transformation by God's unlimited power and unfailing love. Her motto is 'come transparent…leave transformed.'

A servant at heart, she has faithfully served in God's house for over thirty years with a hunger and thirst for God's presence and to know His purposes and plans for her life. In 1999, she was ordained as a minister and as an elder in 2004. In 2007 she was ordained to pastor Kingdom Life Ministries International, a wonderful group of committed servants of God. In 2014, Doretha was ordained as a five-fold evangelist to reach nations with the transforming gospel of Jesus Christ. Her unique style of ministry has helped many be perfected through the teaching and preaching of the Word of God.

While serving as Senior Pastor of Kingdom Life Ministries Intl, Father God has expanded their territory to include Life Skills Institute, her private practice as a Christian Professional Therapist. She is a

Chicago Public Schools retiree, a Licensed Clinical Social Worker (LSCW) in three states, a Certified Alcohol and Drug Counselor (CADC) and holds a Master of Arts in Social Service Administration (MASSA). This woman is a true gift from God to His Kingdom.

Doretha has committed her life to trusting in the Lord's guidance as she obeys His command in Matthew 6:33 (Amp), "But seek (aim at and strive after) ye first of all His kingdom and His righteousness (His way of doing and being right), and then all these things taken together will be given you besides." She is living proof that this Word is true!

www.ingramcontent.com/pod-product-compliance
Lightning Source LLC
Chambersburg PA
CBHW071726090426
42738CB00009B/1890